Law and Ethics in Pharmacy Practice

FASTtrack

Law and Ethics in Pharmacy Practice

Ruth Rodgers
Clinical Lecturer in Pharmacy Practice, Law and Ethics,
Medway School of Pharmacy,
Universities of Kent and Greenwich, UK

Catherine Dewsbury
Clinical Lecturer in Pharmacy Practice, Law and Ethics,
Medway School of Pharmacy,
Universities of Kent and Greenwich, UK

Andrew Lea
Lecturer in Pharmacy Practice,
Medway School of Pharmacy,
Universities of Kent and Greenwich, UK

Pharmaceutical Press
London • Chicago

Published by Pharmaceutical Press

1 Lambeth High Street, London SE1 7JN, UK
1559 St. Paul Avenue, Gurnee, IL 60031, USA

© Pharmaceutical Press 2010

(PP) is a trade mark of Pharmaceutical Press
Pharmaceutical Press is the publishing division of the Royal Pharmaceutical
Society of Great Britain

First published 2010

Typeset by Thomson Digital, Noida, India
Printed in Great Britain by TJ International, Padstow, UK

ISBN 978 0 85369 885 2

FSC
Mixed Sources
Product group from well-managed
forests and other controlled sources
Cert no. SGS-COC-2482
www.fsc.org
© 1996 Forest Stewardship Council

Contents

Introduction to the *FASTtrack* series

FASTtrack is a new series of revision guides created for undergraduate pharmacy students. The books are intended to be used in conjunction with textbooks and reference books as an aid to revision to help guide students through their exams. They provide essential information required in each particular subject area. The books will also be useful for pre-registration trainees preparing for the Royal Pharmaceutical Society of Great Britain's (RPSGB's) registration examination, and to practising pharmacists as a quick reference text.

The content of each title focuses on what pharmacy students really need to know in order to pass exams. Features include*:
- concise bulleted information
- key points
- tips for the student
- multiple choice questions (MCQs) and worked examples
- case studies
- simple diagrams.

The titles in the *FASTtrack* series reflect the full spectrum of modules for the undergraduate pharmacy degree.

Titles include:
Complementary and Alternative Medicine
Managing Symptoms in the Pharmacy
Pharmaceutical Compounding and Dispensing
Pharmaceutics: Dosage Form and Design
Pharmaceutics: Drug Delivery and Targeting
Pharmacology
Physical Pharmacy (based on Florence & Attwood's *Physicochemical Principles of Pharmacy*)
Therapeutics

There is also an accompanying website which includes extra MCQs, further title information and sample content: www.fasttrackpharmacy.com.

If you have any feedback regarding this series, please contact us at feedback@fasttrackpharmacy.com.

*Note: not all features are in every title in the series.

Preface

Pharmacy law and ethics rarely raise excitement amongst pharmacists or pharmacy technicians and yet along with the knowledge of drugs and their uses they form the foundation upon which pharmacy practice is built.

Pharmacy is a combination of science and art; the science requires painstaking attention to detail and accuracy, whilst the art involves the caring skills utilised for the benefit of patients and the public generally.

Legislation is generally couched in legal terminology that makes it difficult to understand; it tends to be general rather than provide specific information that says what must be done. In many cases its interpretation is open to discussion and yet the penalties for failing to comply can be severe. Ignorance of law is not an acceptable defence; however much depends upon knowledge of the impact of precedence and interpretation. Understanding how laws are made, how they come into effect and how they are enforced is key to understanding their importance to the pharmacist practitioner. It is from this basis that this book aims to cover key legislation affecting pharmacy.

Whilst law is seen as black and white – you either comply with it or you don't – ethics is often viewed as shades of grey. Professional ethics is all about doing the 'right' thing – the challenge is to balance the 'rights' of individuals and organisations – and often results in solving challenging situations and dilemmas. Like legislation, reference to a code of ethics rarely provides practitioners with the answer to their specific quandary. The approach taken with this publication is to cover the four basic healthcare ethical principles as set out by Beauchamp and Childress (2008) and build upon these towards an understanding of ethics specific to pharmacy.

Note: this is an exciting time for pharmacy, with many legal and professional changes either having recently occurred or just about to happen. The facts contained in this book were checked at the time of writing; however the authors cannot be held responsible for changes that have occurred since going to press.

Reference

Beauchamp TL, Childress JF. *Principles of Biomedical Ethics*, 6th edn. New York: Oxford University Press, 2008.

About the authors

After qualifying, RUTH RODGERS was a community pharmacy manager and subsequently a regional manager. In 1992 she was appointed Head of Ethics at the Royal Pharmaceutical Society of Great Britain where her responsibilities included review and implementation of the Code of Ethics for pharmacists and secretary to the Ethics Infringement Committee. She has been a fellow of the Institute of Pharmacy Management and was its general secretary for several years. She spent 4 years as a public health pharmacist within the NHS in Kent having specific responsibility for community pharmacy services and contracts covering 260 pharmacy contractors.

She joined Medway School of Pharmacy as a clinical lecturer in pharmacy practice, law and ethics at its inception in 2004 and has been responsible for the development of undergraduate teaching at all levels in these subjects. She has published a number of articles in pharmacy journals; her main areas of interest are pharmacy law, ethics and service development.

CATHERINE DEWSBURY has considerable experience of pharmacy practice in a number of areas. After periods of time in hospital and community pharmacy she was appointed to a position as pharmaceutical officer at the Department of Health with specific interests in pharmaceutical public health. This was followed by a period as the Clinical Governance Pharmacist for the Royal Pharmaceutical Society of Great Britain. Before moving to the Medway School of Pharmacy as a clinical lecturer in pharmacy practice she had undertaken a key role as project pharmacist for the National Patient Safety Agency as well as continuing in the role of lead pharmacist for community pharmacy services in Kent.

She has qualifications in public health as well as philosophy and ethics. Her particular interests include patient safety, policy and the future roles for pharmacists.

After a 2-year period as a practising pharmacist and teacher practitioner ANDREW LEA is now a lecturer in pharmacy practice at the Medway School of Pharmacy. After qualifying he worked for a number of years for major multiple retail pharmacy bodies, undertaking various pharmacist and managerial roles. He is committed to training and development and has wide experience of this, ranging from counter assistant through pre-registration pharmacist and overseas pharmacist training. Andrew has a keen interest in pharmacy law and practice, especially with regard to clinical governance and the improvement of pharmacy standards.

For some time he served as the pharmacy representative member of Ashford primary care trust professional executive committee. In addition to his community pharmacy training and development role he teaches pharmacy practice at all levels of the MPharm programme at Medway.

Introduction

Pharmacy practice involves the assessment of facts relating to specific circumstances in the light of the moral and professional values of the individuals concerned. Many of the facts will relate to clinical evidence but in addition this will be applied against a background of legislation and good practice. The values expressed will have developed through belonging to a society and more specifically to a subgroup of practitioners within the healthcare professions.

The application of these facts and values enables the individual practitioner to make decisions and to give reasons for the actions taken. The law, as well as the professional regulation body and the public, will demand reasons for professional actions. This book sets out revision notes on many aspects of law and professional ethics that are covered during the undergraduate curriculum at Schools of Pharmacy in Britain. However, law and ethics are not static. This means that students, and eventual practitioners, need to remain alert throughout their professional life for changes and amendments to each and to be aware of how these will affect and impact on their chosen area of practice.

Legislation and ethical principles are the backbone against which clinical practice takes place. Legislation sets out the rules or structure for what we can do and what we are not allowed to do and outlines the consequences of breaking the rules. Every pharmacist has a duty to practise lawfully and the sanctions for failing to do so can be harsh. The consequences of breaking the rules governing professional practice can include criminal prosecution resulting in a fine or, in more serious cases, imprisonment, as well as removal of the right to continue to practise (removal from the register). Pharmacists, as well as adhering to legislation, are required to follow the requirements of the Code of Ethics and other guidance and standards set out by the professional regulator.

When applying clinical knowledge in practice patients and the public will rightly wish to assume that the knowledge will be up to date, relevant and safe. Early legislation relating to pharmacy was concerned with prohibiting harmful practices, bringing conformity to arrangements for the supply of medicines and restricting authority to a few types of practitioner. Pharmacists were all required to achieve a set standard of education, to register with the Royal Pharmaceutical Society of Great Britain and pay an annual retention fee in order to be able to continue to practise. The sale and supply of medicines were restricted by legislation, as was the setting-up of a retail pharmacy business.

More recent legislative trends have been towards increasing the rights of the patient. Issues such as confidentiality and data protection along with encouraging patient involvement with healthcare decisions have been the subject of legislation.

Other recent changes have allowed pharmacists to utilise their clinical skills to become authorised prescribers as well as dispensers or suppliers of medicines.

A knowledge and understanding of pharmacy legislation are therefore crucial to be able to practise. Pharmacy legislation sets out the framework of rules that govern what we can do legally.

The interpretation of legislation is complex. To do so accurately one must study and practise for many years; even then there is the possibility of legal argument and disagreement, with lawyers quoting different case law decisions to prove their point. The views and interpretations contained in this work are those of the authors as practising pharmacists and lecturers in pharmacy practice. Note of interpretations, as set out in the documents referenced, has been taken and every attempt has been made to ensure that these are accurate and up to date. Despite these efforts we must include a disclaimer to the effect that this revision book is not an authoritative interpretation. The only reliable arbiter of the law is the court and legal system.

In the British legal system there is a presumption of innocence. It is up to the prosecution, usually the Crown Prosecution Service, to put the complaint and prove guilt unless a defendant admits guilt at an early stage. Cases alleging breach of the law are considered in the legal courts. The majority will be dealt with in the Magistrates Courts where a bench of three lay magistrates will consider the matters alleged (although, particularly in London, a single stipendiary – legally qualified – magistrate may be employed). More serious cases and appeals against Magistrate Court decisions are referred to the Crown Courts where the case or trial will be heard by a legally qualified judge, often with a lay jury.

This book is a revision of law relating to pharmacy practice in England. In many cases this will be the same as the requirements in Wales and, although much will be the same in Scotland, it should be noted that the legal system of this country is fundamentally different to that in England and Wales.

Chapter 1 includes a basic description of law and its implementation in Great Britain.

Chapters 3–8 aim to set out the key issues relating to pharmacy practice that are covered by current legislation, Acts of Parliament or statutory instruments. To be able to appreciate the importance of legislation it is necessary to understand the framework for the development and amendment of those documents. For this reason Chapter 2 sets out to describe the processes by which laws are made and updated as well as touching briefly on how these are enforced.

No work on pharmacy governance would be complete without including some discussion of ethics and morality. Some would say that the values encompassed by these are the background from which the legal processes have developed. Others would say that ethics and morality lie above the basis of the law, imposing additional requirements upon us as we live our lives or carry out our professional practice. In pharmacy we have a Code of Ethics plus many guidance documents. Increasingly, reference to the Code of Ethics and professional guidance is encountered in the rules (statutory or otherwise) that govern the profession and Chapters 9 and 10 consider ethics and its role in pharmacy practice. Issues such as continuing fitness to practise and revalidation, which are embedded in current healthcare policy documents, will be considered along with the purpose of guidance and its status.

chapter 1
Legislation

Overview

Upon completion of this chapter, you should:
- be able to describe how the legislative system works in Great Britain
- be aware of Green Papers, White Papers and Bills
- be able to distinguish between Acts, regulations and rules
- be able to recognise the differences between criminal law, civil law and administrative law
- be able to describe how legislation is amended and the process of keeping legislation relevant
- be able to relate legislation to relevant examples in pharmacy practice.

Laws, policy and practice: a framework

This chapter aims to set out a brief explanation of some of the terms that are often used in connection with the legal framework that surrounds pharmacy practice. These terms, such as policy, law, acts, statutory instruments, regulations and directions, can be confusing. Throughout life as well as in professional practice it is common to hear about Green Papers and White Papers; these affect day-to-day living in society as well as in pharmacy practice. It is not necessary to be an expert in law and legal processes but having a basic knowledge of what each of these terms means and how laws are made will help pharmacists and future pharmacists understand the political and legal framework in which practice takes place.

How the legislative system works

A brief description of the legal system in Great Britain is set out here to provide a background to its purpose and to assist in understanding how the British legal system works in practice, specifically how this relates to the practising pharmacist.

Tips

Legislation doesn't always apply to all the countries that make up the British Isles. It is important to recognise some of the basic differences in the terms used.

- Great Britain consists of Scotland, England and Wales.
- In addition the United Kingdom (UK) includes Northern Ireland.
- The British Islands include the Isle of Man and the Channel Islands but not the Republic of Ireland.
- The term 'British Isles' is geographic rather than political and consists of many islands off the north-west coast of Europe, including the whole of Ireland, the Scilly Islands and many others.

Exercise

List three pieces of legislation that affect medicines and/or pharmacy.

Decide whether you think each piece you have chosen is an Act, regulation or statutory instrument.

Now read the chapter below and review your decision.

Laws

الا لتزام

All pharmacists and pharmacy owners have to abide by the laws relating to the running of a pharmacy. But where do these laws come from? Which are the laws that have to be followed and what are the consequences of not abiding by them?

This book sets out a short revision of the main laws relating to pharmacy practice. These include those relating to opening and running a pharmacy and providing services to patients under the National Health Service (NHS) contractual framework, as well as looking at the roles and responsibilities of a pharmacist, the NHS contractual framework (if working in a pharmacy on an NHS list – see Chapter 6) and also laws relating to procuring, prescribing, supplying, administering and disposing of medicines. These practices are mostly set out in laws – Acts of Parliament, regulations and directions. Many of the current rules governing pharmacy originated in Acts of Parliament that might have been introduced more than 30 years ago, for example the Misuse of Drugs Act 1971, or even 40 years ago, such as the Medicines Act 1968. Despite their vintage, these laws are still relevant today and age alone does not make them obsolete. Some of the laws are specific to pharmacy, for example, The Pharmacy and Pharmacy Technicians Order 2007. Others, like the NHS Act 1977, by their nature relate to and include pharmacy practice. Yet others can affect what pharmacists do and how they do it but their titles are not directly related to pharmacy or medicines. Examples of these include the Data Protection Act 1998 and the Health and Safety at Work Act 1974. Details of how these two acts relate to and have an impact on the pharmacy profession are set out in Chapter 7.

Laws can affect single individual countries within the UK, such as Scotland or Northern Ireland. They may cover more than one country, for example England and Wales, the whole of Great Britain or even the whole of the UK (Great Britain and Northern Ireland). In terms of pharmacy, there is a separate NHS contractual framework for each of Scotland and Northern Ireland with a single contractual framework jointly covering England and Wales. The principal legislation about medicines, the Medicines Act 1968, is called reserved legislation, which means that it covers all four of the countries making up the UK.

Since the UK is a member of the European Union (EU), many of the laws that are developed in the UK are based on or implement laws that are relevant Europewide. An example of European law that directly affects pharmacy is the European directives that govern how pharmacy is taught at undergraduate level in universities, directive 85/432/EEC and directive 85/433/EEC. These directives set the indicative curriculum that covers undergraduate education and the accreditation of schools of pharmacy to deliver the Masters in Pharmacy (MPharm) programme. In this instance the European laws (directives) recognised the existing British legislation set out in the Pharmacy Act 1954 and in the

Supplemental Charter of the then professional regulatory body, the Pharmaceutical Society of Great Britain (PSGB) – see Chapter 9. Further European directives deal with arrangements for the mutual recognition of pharmacists to permit them to move and work in all EU countries, with each country agreeing to accept other countries' certificates and qualifications.

Criminal law, civil law and administrative law

In the UK, the source of law is the statutes or Acts passed by the UK Parliaments. The understanding of what these laws actually mean in practice is achieved through study and interpretation, which is carried out by lawyers, mostly through the application of case law. Case law involves looking back at and reviewing judgements made on previous cases relating to similar circumstances to see how the law has been applied and interpreted. The decision containing the interpretation in a legal judgement for a specific case is called a precedent. The precedent set in an earlier case will generally be followed in subsequent cases of a similar nature unless it has been successfully challenged in the courts.

There are three main areas of law within the British legal system: criminal law, civil law and administrative law. There is also a branch of law relating to the church; however, as this has no relevance to pharmacy practice it will not be covered in this publication. The judicial systems in the UK differ among its member countries, with England and Wales following one system. Scotland and Northern Ireland have their own different systems.

Criminal law is that which relates to maintaining social order and protecting the community as a whole. If these laws are broken the individual concerned can be arrested and prosecuted by representatives of the state through the criminal judicial system. In England and Wales this often means attending a court, usually the Magistrates Court, although more serious cases will be referred to the Crown Court. As the name suggests, cases in the Magistrates Court are heard by a team of magistrates (lay people) who are also known as Justices of the Peace. They are not legally qualified but do undergo regular training following selection and normally work as a team of three, known as a 'bench', along with a legally qualified Magistrates Court clerk. Magistrates deal with at least 90% of all criminal cases.

A legally qualified judge, a highly qualified lawyer, oversees Crown Courts, often with a jury consisting of 12 lay citizens who have been randomly selected from the local electoral list. The jurors' role is to listen to the facts of the case and the evidence presented and, following discussion in private, come to a conclusion about whether the accused person is innocent or guilty. If the verdict is guilty, the judge then decides on and announces the penalty to be imposed.

In criminal law an accused individual is presumed to be innocent until proven to be guilty. The level of proof required in criminal law is that the guilt has been proven 'beyond reasonable doubt'. The penalties for breaking criminal law include fines and imprisonment. Scotland also operates a two-tier court system, with the Solemn Courts dealing with the more serious cases and the Summary Courts the less serious ones. There is a third option available to Scottish courts, in relation to the finding of 'not proven' in addition to the findings of 'guilty' and 'not guilty'.

An example of criminal law that relates to pharmacy practice is the Medicines Act 1968. Under this legislation pharmacists can be, and have been, prosecuted in the criminal courts for a number of offences but most commonly for failing to supervise the sale of pharmacy medicines from registered retail pharmacy businesses under section 52 of this Act. The penalties imposed have usually been significant fines.

Civil law relates to issues or disputes between individuals or corporate bodies. An individual or organisation will make a claim or sue the other person – the defendant – in relation to wrongs or harm caused to them and the penalties can be a monetary award or damages. Cases are considered in the county courts or the High Court (in Scotland most cases are heard through the Sheriff Court). These county courts also deal with family matters, such as divorce, adoption and domestic violence. Civil cases have to be proved 'on balance of probability': this is a lesser standard of proof than is required for criminal cases and approximates to a more than 50% probability that the defendant is guilty. So far as pharmacy is concerned claims for negligence, for example that harm was caused to a patient by the actions of the pharmacist, would be dealt with through the civil justice system.

Administrative law covers the procedures that are put in place for ensuring that the decision-making processes and systems are regulated. Shortfalls in relation to administrative justice are dealt with through tribunals and inquiries. It is unlikely that many pharmacists would become involved in this aspect of legislation; however, it does have an impact on the way the professional regulator is set up and how it deals with misbehaviour of members. It also relates to the way the NHS is set up, for example to deal with breaches of the NHS pharmaceutical services contract through its tribunals.

The next section deals with the process by which an idea becomes law in Parliament. It includes a brief description of the various steps involved, including the consultation on proposals and process of lobbying prior to acceptance of legislation.

Policy ideas, Green Papers and White Papers: where does policy come from?

Changing legislation often starts with a problem that needs to be solved. Alternatively it may result from an intention of politicians and civil servants to change something. This change may be required for a number of reasons, for example because of a problem, as a result of the findings of research, or resulting from a negotiation on NHS payments or terms of service such as the pharmacy contractual framework.

Before something can be changed there has to be an agreement that a change is needed and/or a plan for change. A pharmacy example of such a plan would be an agreement to place more emphasis on clinical pharmacy practice rather than dispensing within the NHS pharmaceutical services provided from pharmacies. Such an agreement or plan is called a policy. 'Policy' is a term that is used in many organisations but most often used by political parties and governments.

Policy development looks at ideas and identifies problems before seeking to set out options and consider the risks and benefits of potential solutions. Any exploration of such problems and possible solutions will look at the potential consequences of doing nothing and doing something. A number of actions or possible actions will be outlined with ideas (intended outcomes and possibly unintended outcomes) about the consequences of the various options. The various options may be prioritised and someone in authority in an organisation (in the case of government this will be a minister in the government department to which the policy relates) will have to make a decision as to which option is preferred. Sometimes options are relatively straightforward and easy, a decision is made and the issue becomes policy.

Green Papers and White Papers

On other occasions the ideas or solutions to a particular problem need further discussion, or even formal consultation, with the people or groups directly or indirectly affected by these proposals for change. The ideas are often brought together in the form of a discussion document. When the discussion document is referring to a discussion on the development of British government policy it is commonly referred to as a Green Paper.

Green papers are often the precursor to a statement of policy setting out a proposal for a way forward. Documents from government departments such as the Department of Health (see subsequent paragraphs) which set out a firm statement of policy or a set of objectives for a future strategic direction are called White Papers.

Where the White Paper is going to result in new legislation being laid before Parliament, this is called a 'Command White Paper'. A pharmacy example of a Command White Paper is the April 2008 publication *Pharmacy in England – Building on Strengths, Delivering the Future*. This White Paper provided a future strategic direction for pharmacy, particularly community pharmacy in England (DH 2008).

Pharmacy in England has already resulted in legislative changes in pharmacy regulation, for example, the arrangements for setting up the new regulatory body for pharmacy, the General Pharmaceutical Council or GPhC (see Chapter 8). Changes currently before Parliament will result in new mechanisms for permitting community pharmacies to provide services under the NHS contractual framework through the changes to pharmaceutical needs assessment requirements set out in the Health Act 2009 (see Chapter 5 for details of the Health Acts).

Public consultations

When a Green Paper, or later a piece of draft legislation, is put out to public consultation, a time limit of at least 12 weeks is set in order to allow interested parties, groups or individuals to put forward their comments. All the comments received are then considered and any amendments made in the draft document before taking the next steps. For a Green Paper the next step would be to move towards it becoming a White Paper; for a draft piece of legislation this would be to put it forward to Parliament with the aim of it becoming law.

Bills and Acts of Parliament

Once there is an agreed policy (Command White Paper) it is time to consider implementation. If that implementation requires a change to the law a whole new process starts. The first part of the process of developing legislation is to draw up, or prepare, a Bill. A Bill is a draft piece of legislation that will be given to Parliament for consideration before it becomes a law or an Act of Parliament. Bills can start in either of the two chambers of the Houses of Parliament.

The principal law-making chamber of the UK Parliament is the House of Commons. This is made up of elected individuals or representatives from geographic areas or localities who are called Members of Parliament (MPs). General elections are held in the UK approximately every 5 years. Members of the House of Commons are elected by a first-past-the-post voting system (that means the person with the largest number of votes is the winner). Voting at general elections is by members of the public aged 18 years or more and living in the particular locality. For the purposes of elections the country is divided into localities called constituencies. The House of Commons currently has 646 MPs, each representing a single constituency. Between general elections a new MP may be elected in a single constituency by-election to replace an existing post-holder. This can be to replace an MP who dies or who stands down for any reason.

At the general election local people vote to select their local MPs to represent their interests. Most MPs are linked to one of the main three political parties: Conservative, Labour or Liberal Democrat, although there are some smaller parties such as the Scottish Nationalists. A very small number of MPs are independent: this means they are not linked to a particular party. The government is made up of MPs from the party with the largest number of MPs. The Prime Minister is usually the leader of the political party with the largest number of MPs. It is the Prime Minister who selects and appoints ministers for various roles in government (see below).

The second house or chamber of the Houses of Parliament is the House of Lords. This is sometimes called the Upper House due to it being the older of the two houses and because it is made up of peers of the realm. Until the 20th century all members of this house held their position due to heredity; that is, individuals had inherited their title and their right to sit in the House of Lords through their family. This situation changed when life peers (lords for their lifetime) were appointed. Now life peers make up the majority in the House of Lords. This means that Britain, as one of the oldest democracies in the world, has an unelected Upper House. But why have two Houses? In fact most democratic countries have two Houses, both of which are usually elected – one house leads the legislative process and the other, in this case the House of Lords, is a modifying chamber to ensure issues of accountability and fairness.

A Bill can start its progress towards becoming law in either of the two Houses of Parliament. Whichever House the process begins in, the steps required for a Bill to become law are similar. A Bill goes through several steps, commencing with the first reading then publication. This is followed by a second reading before progressing to the committee stage (or Grand Committee if taking place in the House of Lords) and then report. After this it will go to a third reading before being put forward for royal assent. It is at this stage, when the Queen gives her royal assent, that the Bill becomes an Act of Parliament and is adopted as law. The royal assent is generally a formality and the monarch does not usually become involved, with agreement being an automatic process after the earlier procedures have been completed. Although the Queen has the constitutional right to refuse consent, it has been more than 200 years since a monarch has done this.

During the process of a Bill becoming law, members of both the House of Commons and the House of Lords have the opportunity to debate the Bill. This debate and discussion takes place in the chambers of Parliament and in committees, as a result of which changes might be proposed and agreed. The aim of the debates is to clarify understanding of what the various different clauses and schedules mean and the conditions or situations to which these may apply. Discussions on the minute details of the Bill usually take place within a committee made up of a small group of MPs appointed across the political parties. The members of a committee are appointed in proportion to the numbers of MPs in each political party to maintain representation of the electing public. This means that the government, that is the political party with the largest number of elected MPs, will make up the largest share of the politicians on the committee. This whole process of moving between readings in the House and committees is completed with publication of the Act of Parliament. As a result of this the Bill ceases to exist (or be needed) as it has become an Act (law). Acts of Parliament are rarely implemented immediately; there is usually a delay to allow for changes to practice to be put in place and for the development of professional standards and guidance. There may also be a need to allow time to develop further secondary legislation (see below).

Acts, regulations and rules

Having reviewed the development of an Act of Parliament, this section will now set out an exploration of the differences between primary and secondary legislation, consider why these are important and seek to set out brief guidance to explain some of the language of law.

Acts of Parliament are called 'primary legislation'. This means that they are legislation that will set a framework, often to enable or permit other things to happen. The Act may provide a legal framework that sets an outline or overview of a subject from which more detailed legal guidance may be given in the form of delegated or secondary legislation. Delegated legislation may take the form of regulations, directions, orders or codes. The nature of any delegated legislation is outlined in the Act or primary legislation. For example, the main legislation about controlled drugs is called the Misuse of Drugs Act 1971. This Act gives permission for Parliament to set out regulations about the prescribing, storage and record-keeping requirements concerning medicines covered by the Act. An example of delegated legislation made under this Act is the 2006 amendment number 2 to the Misuse of Drugs Regulations 2001 that sets out the circumstances in which a pharmacist might make a technical amendment to a prescription for a schedule 2 controlled drug. For more details on this regulation, see Chapter 4. Another pharmacy example is the Medicines Act 1968 which is primary legislation and has delegated legislation to set out which medicines are prescription-only (POM), and are known as POM orders, and which medicines can be sold from premises other than pharmacies, the General Sales List. In this case the delegated legislation for POMs is an order, i.e. The Prescription Only Medicines Order. For more detail, see Chapter 2.

KeyPoints

An Act of Parliament may sometimes be referred to as a statute, with delegated or secondary legislation being termed a statutory instrument.

Acts or statutes are given a name that relates to their subject area and the year in which they were granted royal consent.

Statutory instruments are given a designated number as well as the title and year. For example, the regulations covering the arrangements for the supply of controlled drugs on prescription are Statutory Instrument 3998 Misuse of Drugs Regulations 2001 (as amended). The term 'as amended' means that the original 2001 regulations have not been revoked; however, these have been subject to several amendments, all of which need to be noted and taken into account when using the legislation.

An Act of Parliament may stay in force while the regulations made under it may be changed numerous times. This use of secondary legislation explains why, for example, the Medicines Act 1968 can still be relevant to practice over 40 years after it was adopted.

To find out more about UK government policy and legal processes visit www.ukparliament.gov.uk.

Implementation: public spending, government and the Department of Health

This section is about public spending and the government. As this book is about healthcare and specifically pharmacy, the example used here to explain how the government uses public money will be the Department of Health.

In the UK nationally the government collects money from the populace through taxes and also through payments called National Insurance. Both taxes and National Insurance are collected from individuals either from their salaries (through the pay as you earn (PAYE) system) or paid directly to Her Majesty's Revenue and Customs by people who are self-employed. These funds make up the public expenditure that is apportioned by the government of the day according to its priorities. These priorities may be defence (armed forces and weapons), policing and home affairs, welfare (benefits and social services), foreign office (diplomacy), education, health and the devolved administrations of Wales, Scotland and Northern Ireland.

The government department called the Department of Health manages the monies allotted by the government to pay for healthcare services in England. The Department of Health has a number of offices in London and in Leeds. Its main office is in Richmond House in Whitehall, London (a building often seen in the background of television news items relating to government health policy). The Department of Health website states that its main purpose is to 'improve the health and wellbeing of people in England'.

As one of the main government departments, the Department of Health has six ministers, five of whom are politicians elected to the House of Commons by their local community and appointed to ministerial posts by the Prime Minister. The sixth minister is a member of the House of Lords who is appointed by the Prime Minister to be the lead spokesperson for health matters in the Upper House. The most senior minister in the department is the Secretary of State for Health and he/she is a member of the Cabinet. The Cabinet is the group of most senior ministers and, along with the Prime Minister, it forms the 'executive committee' of government. Within the Department of Health the next tier down from the Secretary of State for Health are the Ministers of State for public health, health services and care services. Finally there are two parliamentary undersecretaries (the most junior ministers), one of whom is a member of the House of Lords.

The ministers' roles are to provide political leadership in a government department or specific areas within a department, for example in relation to public health issues. Civil servants, the paid employees whose appointments are not related to political parties (see below), run the department on a managerial basis. The ministers give political strategic direction and objectives for the areas for which they are responsible and agree resources for their department by negotiation with the Chancellor of the Exchequer. The Chancellor is the government lead on matters relating to spending public money. Ministers with a department lead the decisions on spending priorities and political direction. They are accountable to Parliament.

Civil servants

Whilst ministers are politicians, the majority of the people who work for the Department of Health are career civil servants. Civil servants in the UK are apolitical. This means that they work for the government of the day irrespective of that government's political party. At general elections the government may change but the civil service remains unchanged. This is different from many other countries where the public servants are changed when a new political party takes power. Civil servants in the UK come from a wide variety of backgrounds and their speciality is policy development and implementation. There are generic civil service skills that can be applied across policy areas and between departments. So, in a department like the Department of Health, most of the civil servants will not have healthcare provision experience, nor will they be healthcare professionals. However, due to the specialist nature of healthcare services and the differing roles, regulatory structures and codes of ethics of the various healthcare professions, the Department of Health employs a significant number of healthcare professionals as professional civil servants. These healthcare professionals work alongside the career civil servants to provide a professional perspective on any policy development and to ensure such developments are not in conflict with professional codes of ethics and standards. Even healthcare professionals at a more junior level in the Department of Health have opportunities to promote the changes and developments in professional practice through the application of best practice and the incorporation of research evidence into policy development.

Chief professional officers

The Department of Health has six chief professional officers, one each for the professions of medicine, nursing, dentistry and pharmacy, one for the allied health professions and one for healthcare scientists. These chief professional officer civil servants are leaders in their profession and provide expert advice to other civil servants and to ministers. The most established of these chief professional officers' roles is that of the chief medical officer. The first of these was appointed in 1847 to advise on the cholera outbreak that affected the country that year. Each year the chief medical officer produces a report on healthcare services and needs of the population called *On the State of the Public Health* (Donaldson 2009).

The chief professional officer for pharmacy is called the chief pharmaceutical officer and is the most senior adviser to ministers on matters relating to pharmacy practice.

National clinical directors or healthcare tsars

In addition to chief professional officers, the Department of Health has a number of national clinical directors (NCDs). These experts are referred to as tsars and are specialists in their particular field of practice. National clinical directors/tsars are employed part time at the Department of Health and spend the rest of their working week undertaking their own clinical practice. The term 'tsar' was a title given historically to the leader of all Russians. However in recent years the title 'tsar' has been used to indicate someone who is in a position of high authority in a particular area. In healthcare terms national clinical directors are senior professional leaders and they are considered to hold positions of authority in the NHS. One of the most senior advisory committee that advises the Department of Health is the Medical Board, a committee of national clinical directors and other senior civil servants. The medical director for the NHS chairs this board.

The national clinical director's role is to provide professional leadership to practitioners in their areas of practice. Additionally, possibly their more important role is to be a critical friend to civil servants and ministers. A critical friend provides honest, grounded advice on new proposals and on the impact of existing proposals on practice in the NHS. By providing this advice the NCDs give policy-makers an NHS employee or contractor viewpoint as well as a specialist's opinion on how policy is affecting practitioners and patients. This role is vital as many of the policy-makers are not healthcare professionals themselves and even those who are have often been away from day-to-day clinical practice for a number of years.

Most of the national clinical directors are doctors – the only ones who are not doctors are the two pharmacy NCDs. These two pharmacy national clinical directors were both appointed in 2008, one for primary care, including community pharmacy, and the other for secondary care or hospital pharmacy.

Head of pharmacy

In addition to the chief pharmaceutical officer and the two pharmacy national clinical directors, the Department of Health has a role for a head of pharmacy. The head of pharmacy is a position for a career civil servant.

Tips

Primary legislation, the Acts of Parliament, sets the framework for the preparation of the secondary delegated legislation known as statutory instruments. These can be regulations, orders or directives.

Criminal laws are developed to encourage and support safe and orderly living for all citizens and are enforced by the state through the criminal courts, Magistrates' and Crown Courts. The defendant is innocent until proved guilty 'beyond reasonable doubt' and the penalties imposed can be fines or imprisonment.

Civil laws relate to contracts between individuals who can sue for breach of that contract. The court can award damages to the injured party if the defendant is proven guilty 'on the balance of probabilities'.

The process of developing new laws in response to strategic political policy takes place in the Houses of Parliament through preparation, debate and consultation on various discussion papers – the Green and White Papers which precede the drawing-up of a Bill. Once approved, the Bill will become the Act of Parliament.

Policy documents, the subsequent papers and Bills are developed by the relevant government department; the department dealing with pharmacy matters is the Department of Health.

This person is the lead on the policy development and legislative changes needed to implement pharmacy policy. The head of pharmacy is also responsible for leading the Department of Health negotiations on the terms of service, reimbursement and remuneration under the NHS contractual framework for pharmaceutical services (see Chapter 6).

The chief pharmaceutical officer, the head of pharmacy and the pharmacy national clinical directors have a small team of pharmacists advising them within the Department of Health and work closely with the chief pharmaceutical officers in Wales, Scotland and Northern Ireland. Additionally the head of pharmacy heads a large team of career civil servants working on pharmacy policy, including the community pharmacy contractual framework and changes to the regulatory framework for pharmacists and pharmacy technicians (see Chapter 8).

Self-assessment

1. Describe two key differences between criminal and civil law.
2. How many chambers are there in the UK Parliament?
3. Where in the UK are these government chambers situated?
4. How many Members of Parliament sit in the House of Commons?
5. Who is the current Secretary for State for Health?
6. How many health ministers are there in the main government department?
7. Name the current Health Minister with responsibility for pharmacy.
8. There are a number of chief professional officers who are civil servants providing advice to ministers. List three of the chief professional officers' posts and name the current holders of these jobs.

References

Department of Health. *Pharmacy in England – Building on Strengths, Delivering the Future*. London: Department of Health, 2008.
Donaldson L. *On the State of the Public Health*. London: Department of Health, 2009.

Further reading

Appelbe GE, Wingfield J. *Dale and Appelbe's Pharmacy Law and Ethics*, 9th edn. London: Pharmaceutical Press, 2009.
Merrills J, Fisher J. *Pharmacy Law and Practice*. London: Blackwell Science, 2003.
Rogers R, Walters R. *How Parliament Works*, 6th edn. London: Pearson Longman, 2006.

chapter 2
The Medicines Act 1968

Overview

Upon completion of this chapter, you should be able to:
- describe the background leading to the introduction of the Medicines Act 1968
- understand the licensing system for medicinal products
- understand and describe the arrangements for lawful operation of a retail pharmacy business and the requirements for registration of pharmacy premises
- demonstrate knowledge of the legal requirements for the sale, supply and administration of medicines
- demonstrate awareness of the following legal terms: responsible pharmacist, supervision and personal control; and to discuss their implication in practice.

Introduction and background to medicines legislation

Until the introduction of the Medicines Act 1968 most medicines were regulated as poisons. This acknowledges clearly the fact that in having a medicinal effect the compound – chemical, mineral or plant derivative – could also be expected to have a potentially harmful effect. Earlier regulation did not guarantee efficacy or safety of a medicine; rather established use, manufacturers' claims and sometimes even folklore determined this.

During the early to mid part of the 20th century, the synthetic development of drugs with medicinal properties was accelerating. The pharmaceutical industry and researchers were spending more and more time (and money) looking to develop medicines that would treat and prevent the medical scourges of the time. Most medicines, other than 'dangerous drugs' (which were covered by the Dangerous Drugs Act 1920, as amended), were classified as poisons under the Pharmacy and Poisons Act 1933. Newly developed antibiotics and other therapeutic substances were classified under the Therapeutic Substances Act 1956. Evidence-based practice and extensive clinical trials were not standard practice. One of the key developments that led to the Medicines Act being drawn up was the thalidomide tragedy. In the late 1950s, the Distillers Company had widely marketed the drug,

Distaval, following its introduction in Germany in 1957. This was claimed to be an effective sleeping tablet and antiemetic, and was advertised as completely safe with no side-effects. It was prescribed to pregnant women throughout the world to alleviate symptoms of morning sickness during the early stages of pregnancy. Unfortunately premarketing tests had been insufficient to determine its safety and eventually an increased incidence of babies born with phocomelia (hands and feet attached directly to the body or with reduced limbs and other defects) was noticed. These birth defects are now associated with the use of, and indeed are often referred to as, 'thalidomide'.

KeyPoint

A medicinal product is defined as substances or combinations of substances which either prevent or treat disease in human beings or are administered to human beings with a view to making a medical diagnosis or to restore, correct or modify physiological functions in humans.

A review of the processes and legislation covering the introduction and marketing of all medicinal products followed and, in 1968, the Medicines Act was adopted to cover the processes for marketing, manufacture and supply of medicines within Great Britain and Northern Ireland. At the same time legislation was being developed in Europe. In time the Medicines Act 1968 has been aligned with the Europewide legislation and directives (currently directives 2001/83/EC and 2001/82/EC as amended for human and veterinary medicines respectively).

The Act set up a process of licensing for all products for which a medicinal claim is made. The Medicines Control Agency, now superseded by the Medicines and Healthcare products Regulatory Authority (MHRA), was established under this legislation. A European counterpart, the European Medicines Agency (EMEA), operates a centralised Europewide marketing authorisation for medicines for human and veterinary (animal) use (regulation (EC) no. 726/2004).

The Medicines Act 1968 is prescriptive (that is, 'not enabling') legislation; it makes it unlawful to sell or supply any medicinal products unless in a circumstance when an exemption exists. These exemptions include the supply of medicines against a prescription provided by an authorised prescriber and the retail sale of medicines included on the General Sales List (GSL). These exemptions will be covered later in this chapter.

An application for a licence or a marketing authorisation is made to the MHRA or EMEA which will evaluate the information obtained from the various phases of clinical trials (see KeyPoints) and consider issues relating to the safety, quality and efficacy of the product. Efficacy of the product compared to others for similar purposes is not considered, neither is price taken into account.

Evaluation takes into account the nature of the active ingredients, its dosage form, the nature of the disease or condition to be treated, the effective dose that needs to be given, the type of patient and the duration of treatment. The MHRA takes independent expert advice on matters relating to safety, quality and efficacy from medicines advisory bodies appointed under section 4 (S4) of the Medicines Act. Currently this is the Commission on Human Medicines.

Details of the information required for an application are set out in European directive/83/EC. This includes information such as the pharmaceutical form of the product; its medicinal use; containers and labels; summary of product characteristics; details of manufacture and quality control; reports of clinical trials and any adverse reactions.

Evaluating the beneficial effects against the possible harmful effects of any medicine is complex. A high risk-to-benefit ratio may be acceptable in the treatment of terminally ill patients where quality of life might be enhanced. However, a very low risk-to-benefit ratio is expected in the treatment of patients with self-limiting diseases, for the purpose of prophylaxis (prevention) and for illnesses that require lifelong treatment.

Once all phases of the trials have been completed, product data are submitted to the MHRA or EMEA for assessment and, if acceptable, a marketing authorisation for the product will be granted, usually for a period of 5 years. This system of licensing or issuing of marketing authorisation includes postmarketing surveillance. The Yellow Card scheme exists for practitioners and patients to report suspected adverse reactions to medicinal products or combinations of these to the Commission on Human Medicines and the MHRA. These forms can be completed online at www.yellowcard.gov.uk or posted free of charge. Receipt of Yellow Cards is monitored and can trigger the withdrawal of a product from the market if the level of adverse effect noted is deemed to be too high once a product is used in a wider population than in the initial trials. In addition, a system of alerts is in place to deal with safety issues via the MHRA Defective Medicines Report Centre. Issues are graded from 1 to 4 depending on the seriousness of the threat posed to public health. Grade 1 alerts may include the urgent recall, that must reach all practitioners within 24 hours, of a faulty batch of a particular product, ranging through to grade 4, where caution might be advised when using a particular product.

KeyPoints

Licensing

A brief review of the stages involved from discovery of a suspected new medicinal product through to its marketing and postmarketing surveillance:

- Preclinical research and testing
- Phase I trials: tested on up to 100 healthy volunteers to ensure that the product is safe to use in humans and to obtain information on which to base the design of phase II studies
- Phase II trials: several hundred patients exposed to the product to elicit information relating to its action, short-term side-effects and initial effectiveness. This information will also be used to inform the design of the phase III trial
- Phase III trials: may involve up to several thousand patients and aim to generate data about how well the medicine works, the range and type of side-effects and how safe it is likely to be in the general population. This information will also be used to inform labelling and other issues required for the marketed product.

KeyPoint

The marketing authorisation will include the legal category relating to the supply of the medicine. Many new medicines will be limited to supply against a valid prescription but procedures exist for moving medicines between categories depending on additional safety and efficacy data being provided, sometimes only for specific indications. These are the so-called prescription-only medicine (POM) to pharmacy (P) or P to GSL switches.

Medicines may be sold directly from the manufacturer to the retail outlet but more commonly they are supplied via a wholesaler. Any business involved in the wholesale supply of medicinal products must be in possession of a valid wholesale dealer's licence. The wholesale licence ensures that the supply chain is maintained in a secure manner, that any necessary storage conditions are met and that defective products can be dealt with promptly. Wholesale dealing is where a product is sold to purchasers who will, in the course of their business, sell or supply it, or administer it, or cause it to be administered to another person. Anything else is a retail sale; this includes supplies made under a National Health Service (NHS) contract arrangement.

Pharmacies are exempt from the need for a wholesale dealer's licence when supplying other practitioners or pharmacies so long as the value of wholesale transactions is an inconsiderable part of the business. For pharmacies, it is considered that no more than 5% of the total medicines sales will be considered to meet this criterion and therefore no licence would be required. Circumstances where purchases of medicines from pharmacies under wholesaling arrangements might take place include sales to the following practitioners for use in the course of their business: doctors, dentists, midwives, chiropodists, optometrists – see Snell (2009) for details of items which may be supplied.

Sale and supply of medicines

The Medicines Act 1968 prohibits the sale or supply of medicinal products unless an exemption applies. It defines two classes of medicinal products for human use, and by default sets up a third. These are: POM, GSL medicines and P medicines.

POMs are those that are listed in the Prescription Only Medicines (Human Use) Order 1997 as amended. This is an order made under the primary legislation, the Medicines Act 1968, and is subjected to amendments from time to time. POMs can usually only be legally sold or supplied from a pharmacy against a valid prescription issued by an authorised prescriber. Exemptions apply for sales and supplies made by various practitioners to patients under their care, for example by pharmacists or nurses under a patient group direction which specifies the exact circumstances of the supply. Other exemptions include emergency supplies, supplies by midwives, chiropodists and optometrists – see Snell (2009) for further details.

Most medicinal products that are also classified as controlled drugs under the Misuse of Drugs Act 1971 are also POMs. Exceptions to this rule can include items where the strength of the controlled drug is below a specified limit. When the medicinal product is also a scheduled controlled drug the prescription requirements for that schedule, where these are more stringent, will apply in addition to any POM prescription requirements. For example, a prescription for a schedule 2 controlled drug POM is only valid for 28 days whereas a non-controlled drug POM is valid for 6 months under the Medicines Act 1968 (see Chapter 4 for details).

Although not specified in the Medicines Act 1968, the prescription will also need to contain details of the medicinal product being supplied, such as name and quantity, as well as form and strength, if this is not obvious from the product name.

Note: a fax is not a valid prescription for the supply of a POM under the Medicines Act 1968; the original must be obtained before the medicine is issued to the patient. Special arrangements exist to protect the electronic transmission of prescriptions and ensure that they are authentic and cannot be tampered with.

Records of supplies of POMs made against private prescriptions must be maintained either electronically or in a bound book (Figure 2.1). Whichever method is chosen, the record must contain the following particulars and be available for inspection:
- the date that the sale or supply was made
- the name and address of the patient
- the name, quantity and, usually, the pharmaceutical form and strength, unless this can be determined from the name

KeyPoints

Prescription requirements for a valid prescription-only medicine (POM) prescription
Prescriptions for POMs must be written in ink or otherwise indelible or transmitted in a secure electronic format and:
- include name and address of patient plus age of patient, if under 12 years
- include prescriber's signature in ink (or advanced electronic signature), qualification and address
- be dated and within 6 months of this appropriate date unless it is a repeatable prescription, in which case the first supply must be made within 6 months of the date
- if repeatable, the number of times the supply can be dispensed should be stated; otherwise it cannot generally be repeated more than once (that is, two supplies made in total and the first of these within the 6-month period of validity). An exception is made for oral contraceptives, which can be dispensed a total of six times within the 6-month period from the appropriate date.

Ref. no.			No VAT	VAT
				Page 24
24/1	Monday 17 July 2010			
	John Smith, 7 The Street, Anytown			
	Rx Mefloquine 250 mg tabs x 8, once weekly			
	Dr N E Body, 14 July 2010			
	The Surgery, Anytown	£ 20.00		
24/2	Next entry details			

Figure 2.1 Example of an entry in a private prescription register.

- the date on the prescription and the name and address of the prescriber.

For second and subsequent supplies made on a repeatable prescription a reference to the original supply is sufficient.

Except where the prescription is on an NHS form the prescription must be retained at the pharmacy for a period of 2 years from the date of supply (or from the final supply if the prescription was a repeatable one). (For private prescriptions for controlled drugs, a copy must be retained at the pharmacy.) NHS prescriptions are dealt with differently as these are forwarded to the NHS for payment – see Chapter 6 regarding the NHS pharmaceutical contract.

Labelling dispensed prescription-only medicines

Regulations determine the information legally required to be included on the label of dispensed medicines (Medicines for Human Use (Marketing Authorisations etc.) Regulations 1994, as amended). Legal requirements are: the name of the patient for whom the medicine has been prescribed; the date it was dispensed; the name of the product; directions for use; and any precautions for its use. When the item is a liquid product for external use the label must contain the words 'For external use only' within a rectangle. The name and address of the pharmacy and the words 'Keep out of the reach of children' or similar are also required. It is not a legal requirement to include the quantity of medicine or number of dosage units nor to type or computer generate the label – these are professional requirements set by the professional body as good practice. Generally each container of the product should be labelled, although the legislation allows that several containers may be included in an outer, labelled package. It is certainly good practice and feasible with computer labelling systems to label each container to ensure that all the details are available to the patient with each container supplied.

'Appropriate practitioners' identified in the Medicines Act 1968 were originally only doctors, dentists and veterinarians – the so-called 'medical independent prescribers'. They make, and are accountable for, their own prescribing decisions having taken into account aspects such as the patient's details and condition as well as licensed indication for the item prescribed. In more recent years this list of prescribers has been added to with the introduction of non-medical independent prescribers. These include community practitioner nurse prescribers, independent and supplementary prescribing nurses and pharmacists as well as other specified healthcare professionals. These additional groups of practitioners have all been granted authorisation through amendments to the regulations made under the Medicines Act legislation and are dependent upon the individual meeting appropriate training requirements and registration indicating that they are eligible to undertake this role.

Until 2008, prescriptions were only valid for supply of POMs when the practitioner was registered in Great Britain. From the end of 2008 arrangements were agreed across the European Economic Union (EEU) that prescriptions issued by doctors and dentists registered within the EEU and Switzerland would be valid in Britain. Although the supply would be legal, it is subject to the competence of the supplying pharmacist to be able to interpret the prescription and counsel the patients as well as being able to obtain the intended prescribed medicine. Obviously the pharmacist would also have to satisfy him- or herself of the authenticity of the prescriber's qualifications.

Non-medical independent prescribers are authorised to prescribe in their own right. They must assess the patient, prescribe within their own professional capabilities and accept full liability for their decisions and actions in the same way that an independent medical prescriber has to. Not all non-medical independent prescribers are permitted to prescribe controlled drugs; nurse independent prescribers can prescribe from a limited list whereas pharmacist independent prescribers are not permitted to prescribe any. At the time of writing proposals are in place that may amend this situation; current details should be checked for any subsequent changes.

Supplementary non-medical prescribers share the professional liability and decision-making process with an independent prescriber. Patients have to give their agreement to this form of prescribing and the supplementary prescriber is required to prescribe in accordance with a clinical management plan which has been drawn up for the individual patient. The clinical management plan may include controlled drugs, specifies which medicines the supplementary prescriber can prescribe and details the circumstances when referral must be made to the independent prescriber.

Emergency supplies

Emergency situations arise with regard to the need for supplies of POMs when the patient does not have access to a valid prescription and cannot realistically obtain one. The Medicines Act allows for two types of emergency supply of POMs to be made: at the request of the patient, and at the request of an authorised prescriber. Most controlled drugs and some other listed substances may not be supplied as an emergency supply.

For emergency supplies requested by a patient the pharmacist must first have interviewed the patient and be satisfied that an emergency exists and that it is not practical to obtain a prescription. If this is the case and the patient has previously been treated with a POM prescribed by one of the authorised prescribers, the pharmacist may provide up to 30 days' supply of the medicines with exceptions for certain specified packaging and products. The supply will not come under any NHS arrangements and payment may be requested from the patient. The supply must be recorded either on the day it was made or before the end of the next day. Details to be recorded include the date of supply, name and quantity plus form and strength of the medicine, the name and address of the person supplied along with the nature of the emergency. The medicine supplied must be labelled to show the date of supply, the name and quantity plus form and strength of the medicine, the name of the person requesting it along with the name and address of the pharmacy, the words 'Emergency supply' and 'Keep out of the reach of children'.

Emergency supply may also be made at the request of a prescriber when, because of the emergency, it is not practical for the prescription to be provided immediately. The prescriber must undertake to supply the prescription to the supplying pharmacy within 72 hours and the supply cannot be for a scheduled 1, 2 or 3 controlled drug (except phenobarbital or phenobarbital sodium for epilepsy). An entry must be made in the Prescription register on the day of the supply or by the end of the next day. Details required in the register entry include: the date the supply was made as well as the date on the prescription; the name, quantity plus form and strength of the medicine; the name and address of the prescriber requesting the supply; and the name and address of the patient. When the prescription is received the entry should be amended to record the date it was received.

Patient group directions

A patient group direction is a written direction that can permit the supply and administration, or just the administration, of POMs without a prescription in specified circumstances. The direction must have been signed by a doctor or dentist as well as by a pharmacist and a list of persons who are permitted to supply or administer POMs under these arrangements is set out in the regulations. Most circumstances covered by patient group directions relate to services provided and authorised by an NHS body, for example, the administration of pneumococcal vaccine to patients meeting laid-down criteria by pharmacists in a service commissioned by the local primary care organisation. In Scotland, under specific circumstances, the patient group direction may be used to allow emergency supplies of urgent medicines out of hours.

KeyPoints

Legislation governing the supply of medicines under patient group directions includes:
- The Prescription Only Medicines (Human Use) amendment order 2000 (SI 2000/1917)
- The Medicine (Pharmacy and General Sale – Exemption) amendment order 2000 (SI 2000/1919)
- The Medicines (Sale and Supply) (Miscellaneous Provisions) amendment (no. 2) regulations 2000 (SI 2000/1918)

Pharmacy medicines

P medicines are the third of the three classes of medicinal products set in place by the Medicines Act 1968. No specific list of P medicines exists; instead, this class includes all licensed medicines that are not included on the Prescription Only Medicines Order or on the GSL. It also covers medicines that are made in the pharmacy and sold by retail (where none of the ingredients is categorised as a POM or controlled drug), making use of an exemption from licensing granted to pharmacists under section 10 of the Medicines Act.

Section 52 of the Medicines Act 1968 requires that these medicines may only be sold in retail circumstances from a retail pharmacy business that is conducted from registered pharmacy premises. In addition, the sale or supply has to be made by a pharmacist or someone acting under a pharmacist's supervision. The pharmacist must be present on the registered premises at the time of the sale. In practice many P medicines are sold without the supervising pharmacist being specifically aware of an individual sale. Trained medicines counter assistants apply standard operating procedures which specify when to bring to the attention or refer the customer's request to the pharmacist. Often this may be for a newly introduced P medicine, such as orlistat, which became available as a P product in 2009 and requires specific counselling to ensure correct indication and use. Counselling may be the reason for referring other purchases to the pharmacist, such as in the sale of emergency hormonal contraception, whereas potential misuse of opioid-containing pain relievers may be a further reason. Medicines counter assistants must be undertaking or have completed an accredited training to the National or Scottish Vocational Qualification level 2 (NVQ or SVQ) covering pharmacy services.

General Sales List medicines

These are licensed medicinal products specifically listed in the Medicines (Products other than Veterinary Drugs) (General Sales List) Order 1984, as amended. They can be reasonably safely sold or supplied without the need for being sold by a pharmacist or person acting under a pharmacist's supervision. The legislation also specifies certain classifications of medicines that cannot be sold as GSL, such as eyedrops or eye ointments or products containing certain vitamin A or vitamin D compounds.

Many GSL medicines are, like pharmacy medicines, licensed to be sold only in restricted pack sizes, for restricted indications or restricted strengths, formulations and recommended dose.

Some medicinal products may be licensed in each category. For example, with regard to paracetamol, the ordinary 500 mg strength tablets are available in packs of up to 16 tablets as a GSL medicine, no more than two of which can be sold at a time from a non-pharmacy outlet; packs containing 32 tablets are sold as P medicines with a maximum sale of 100 tablets; and, packs of greater than 32 tablets, usually 100, are POM and require a prescription for a legal supply to be made.

The sale of a GSL medicine in its original unopened package can only legally take place from premises that must be able to be closed to exclude the public. Vending machines supplying GSL medicines for sale must meet these criteria. This means that open-market stalls and car boot sales are not permitted to sell or supply any medicines.

Although GSL medicines may be sold or supplied from premises without a pharmacist in control of the business, an anomaly existed where these were sold from a registered pharmacy. The Medicines Act 1968 required there to be a pharmacist in personal control where the business of a registered pharmacy was carried out. This meant that, even though other retail premises could sell GSL medicines without a pharmacist, a pharmacy could not if the pharmacist was not present on the premises. This issue has been addressed through the introduction of significant new legislation, the Medicines (Pharmacies) (Responsible Pharmacist) Regulations 2008, that took effect from October 2009. This permitted the continued sale of GSL medicines from pharmacies during the absence of the 'responsible pharmacist' for a period of up to a maximum of 2 hours a day – see later in this chapter for details.

Register of pharmacy premises

Pharmacy premises are required, under section 75 of the Medicines Act 1968, to be registered with the Royal Pharmaceutical Society or its replacement for regulatory matters, the General Pharmaceutical Council. This is in addition to any requirement to contract with NHS organisations to provide and be paid for contracted and commissioned services. The register is compiled annually and a fee is required to register initially and afterwards, annually, to remain on the register. Registered pharmacies are usually retail pharmacy businesses but may be a hospital pharmacy department. All separate or distinct parts of the premises have to be registered separately and are subject to separate applications in the required format. If ownership of the registered premises changes the registration becomes void after a specified period of time (currently 28 days). The new owner must apply for restoration and the registrar will restore the premises after being satisfied that the new owner is lawfully entitled to conduct a retail pharmacy business.

Ownership of pharmacies

Ownership of pharmacies in Great Britain is restricted to three separate groups as determined in the Medicines Act 1968 section 69, as summarised in the following:
1. A pharmacist, or a partnership of pharmacists where each partner is a pharmacist (in Scotland only at least one of the partners must be a pharmacist)
2. A body corporate where the business is under the management of a superintendent pharmacist who is not superintendent for any other body corporate. The superintendent pharmacist is required to provide the registrar with a signed statement on behalf of the body corporate confirming whether or not he or she is a member of the board
3. A representative of a deceased, bankrupt or mentally ill pharmacist: the pharmacist's name and the representative's address must be notified to the registrar.

In addition, the pharmacy business had to be under the personal control of a pharmacist whose name and certificate must be prominently displayed. This requirement was amended with the introduction of the responsible pharmacist role, which requires that a notice is on display to the public stating the identity and registration number of the responsible pharmacist at that time (see below).

The terms 'pharmacy' and 'chemist' are restricted titles that may only be used lawfully by those conducting a registered pharmacy. Where the pharmacy is owned by a body corporate the restricted title 'chemist' can only be used if the superintendent pharmacist is a member of the board of directors, otherwise it may only be called a pharmacy.

Responsible pharmacist, supervision and personal control

The legal term, 'the responsible pharmacist', set out in the legislative document SI 2008 no. 2789 The Medicines (Pharmacies) (Responsible Pharmacist) Regulations 2008 came into effect from October 2009. This legislation allows retail sales of GSL medicines to continue during the absence from the pharmacy of the designated responsible pharmacist. It allows for a maximum absence of a total of 2 hours in any 24 hours. This legislation replaces the requirement for a pharmacist to be in personal control of a pharmacy in order that the retail pharmacy business could be carried out. The responsible pharmacist has a statutory duty to secure the safe and effective running of the pharmacy.

Normally, each pharmacy is expected to have a designated responsible pharmacist. However the legislation does allow for an eventuality where a single pharmacist may be the responsible pharmacist for more than one retail pharmacy business/premises, in which case the 2-hour absence rule obviously cannot apply. For such an eventuality, regulations would be made which will specify the precise circumstances in which an exception can be made from this general rule.

Every retail pharmacy premises and registered hospital pharmacy is required to operate with a responsible pharmacist and, where a pharmacy has more than one pharmacist working on the premises at any one time, one of these must be designated and recorded as the responsible pharmacist. If the normal responsible pharmacist is on leave or off sick, then the law requires that a different pharmacist is appointed as the responsible pharmacist for that period of time. This could be a locum pharmacist, or another pharmacist who is working in the pharmacy.

The superintendent pharmacist role continues and retail pharmacy businesses carried on by bodies corporate continue to be required to be under the management of a superintendent pharmacist. The responsible pharmacist, where he or she is not the superintendent pharmacist, remains subject to the directions of the superintendent pharmacist.

KeyPoints

Responsible pharmacist records
The responsible pharmacist has to make a record of who the responsible pharmacist is at any time, including when absent. These can be kept in writing or electronically and must be accessible to the owner of the pharmacy, its superintendent pharmacist, the responsible pharmacist and the staff.

The record must include:
- the name and registration number of the responsible pharmacist
- date and time that person became the responsible pharmacist
- date and time that person ceased to be responsible pharmacist
- date and time any absence began and ceased.

The pharmacy owner must ensure that the record of the responsible pharmacist is properly maintained and preserved for not less than 5 years.

The responsible pharmacist is required to establish procedures (if they are not already established), maintain and keep them under review. These must cover arrangements to ensure that medicines are ordered, stored, prepared, sold, supplied, delivered and disposed of in a safe and effective manner and giving advice on medicines.

He or she must also take responsibility for identifying the pharmacy staff who are competent to undertake specific activities. These include keeping records; the arrangements for times when the responsible pharmacist is absent; and the procedures to be followed when there is a complaint or an adverse incident.

One of the key issues under the responsible pharmacist arrangement is the keeping of records.

A notice with the name of the responsible pharmacist, his or her registration number and the fact that the pharmacist is in charge of the pharmacy is to be conspicuously displayed on the premises. These records, and the required notice, replace the Medicines Act requirement to display the registration certificate of the pharmacist in charge on the pharmacy premises, and also the requirement to make an annual return to the professional registration body.

As indicated, the legislation allows the responsible pharmacist to be absent from the pharmacy and for GSL medicines to be sold during this period. This is limited to a maximum of 2 hours per day, irrespective of whether the pharmacy is covered by one or more responsible pharmacists during a 24-hour period. Certain conditions apply for the absence of the responsible pharmacist to be lawful.

KeyPoints

Responsible pharmacist: conditions for lawful absence
During his or her absence the responsible pharmacist must make arrangements to be contactable by the pharmacy staff, and able to return to the pharmacy with reasonable promptness. Where these conditions are not reasonably practical, the responsible pharmacist must arrange for another pharmacist to be available and contactable.

This 2-hour limit for absence will not apply in the exceptional circumstance when the responsible pharmacist is in charge of two pharmacies.

Tips

The Medicines Act 1968 is enforced through the application of regulations and orders. These govern the medicines that are listed in each of the classifications, labelling requirements for manufactured and dispensed prescription-only medicines, amongst other things. Whilst from time to time elements of the Act are replaced, it is more usual that the regulations will be amended.

When dealing with legal issues it is important to keep abreast of current developments. In law, ignorance is not a defence for failing to adhere to legislation.

The Medicines Act 1968 comes under the aspect of law designated as criminal law. This means that a failure to follow its requirements can be dealt with by prosecution and conviction in the criminal courts.

Self-assessment

1. List the various stages a new drug has to go through in order to obtain a marketing authorisation.

2. **Which of the following is not legally required to be included on the label of a dispensed medicine?**
   a. the date of dispensing
   b. the name of the medicinal product
   c. the quantity of medicinal product in the container
   d. the patient's name

3. **Which one of the following is not a requirement for a legally valid prescription for a POM under the Medicines Act 1968?**
   a. the date of prescribing
   b. the name and address of the patient
   c. the date of birth of the patient
   d. the signature of the prescriber

4. **Which of the following combinations of healthcare professionals must sign a patient group direction for the supply of a POM?**
   a. a doctor, dentist and nurse
   b. a doctor, dentist and pharmacist
   c. a doctor, pharmacist and nurse
   d. a dentist, nurse and pharmacist

5. **Which of the following is a POM medicine?**
   a. a manufacturer's packet containing 16 paracetamol 500 mg tablets
   b. a manufacturer's packet containing 50 paracetamol 500 mg tablets
   c. a manufacturer's packet containing 60 paracetamol effervescent tablets
   d. a manufacturer's packet containing 32 paracetamol 500 mg tablets

6. **Which of the following is/are not a GSL medicine?**
   a. a manufacturer's packet containing 16 aspirin 300 mg tablets
   b. a manufacturer's packet containing 6 ranitidine 75 mg tablets
   c. a medicine made in the pharmacy from ingredients that are all GSL
   d. a complementary therapy

7. **List the records that have to be maintained under the 'responsible pharmacist' regulations.**

8. **Which of the following statements is true?**
   a. A pharmacy can have more than one responsible pharmacist at a time.
   b. A responsible pharmacist must be appointed to cover all the hours that a pharmacy is open for business.
   c. The responsible pharmacist replaces the need for a superintendent pharmacist in bodies corporate that own a pharmacy.
   d. The responsible pharmacist is normally able to take responsibility for a maximum of three pharmacies.

9. **Which one of the following is not a circumstance in which an emergency supply can be made of a POM?**
a. at the request of a patient who has previously been prescribed the item by a doctor registered in Britain
b. at the request of a patient who has previously been prescribed the item by a dentist registered in Britain
c. at the request of a patient who has previously been prescribed the item by a doctor registered in France
d. at the request of a patient who has previously been prescribed the item by a dentist registered in the USA

10. **Which of the following accurately completes the sentence, 'A supplementary prescriber ...'?**
a. must only prescribe medicines that have been previously prescribed for the patient by an independent prescriber
b. may prescribe within the guidelines set out in the clinical management plan
c. is not limited to prescribing only the medicines included in the clinical management plan
d. cannot prescribe controlled drugs even if these are included in the clinical management plan.

Reference

Snell M (ed.) *Medicines Ethics and Practice: A Guide for Pharmacists and Pharmacy Technicians*, 33rd edn. London: Pharmaceutical Press, 2009.

Further reading

Anderson S (ed.) *Making Medicines, A Brief History of Pharmacy and Pharmaceuticals*. London: Pharmaceutical Press, 2005.
Appelbe GE, Wingfield J. *Dale and Appelbe's Pharmacy Law and Ethics*. London: Pharmaceutical Press, 2009.
Langley CA, Belcher D. *Applied Pharmaceutical Practice*. London: Pharmaceutical Press, 2009.
Waterfield J. *Community Pharmacy Handbook*. London: Pharmaceutical Press, 2008.
Whalley BJ, Fletcher KE, Weston SE, *et al. Foundation in Pharmacy Practice*. London: Pharmaceutical Press, 2008.

chapter 3

Veterinary Medicines Regulations

Overview

Upon completion of this chapter, you should be able to:
- describe the background leading to the introduction of the Veterinary Medicines Regulations and how these are updated
- demonstrate knowledge of the legal requirements for the sale and supply of veterinary medicines
- define the term 'veterinary medicinal product'
- define the four legal categories of veterinary medicines
- know the requirements for sale and supply, including labelling and record keeping
- understand the requirements of the cascade system for prescribing unlicensed products or products outside their licence.

Introduction

Originally the Medicines Act 1968 covered arrangements for the sale of all medicines, including those for the treatment of animals. For this reason, veterinary surgeons and veterinary practitioners were designated as appropriate practitioners for the purpose of prescribing medicines. In 2005, the existing arrangements were replaced by the Veterinary Medicines Regulations, the first of which came into effect on 1 October of that year. These regulations meet the requirements of the European directive 2001/82/EC (as amended by 2004/28/EC) and bring the UK legislation in line with that of the rest of Europe. The regulations are revoked and remade each year to ensure that they are kept up to date rather than amending them.

Veterinary Medicines Regulations

The regulations relate to medicines supplied in England, Scotland, Wales and Northern Ireland for animals, which includes birds, reptiles, fish, molluscs, crustaceans and bees.

The regulations define what is meant by the term 'veterinary medicinal product' (VMP) and

Tip

A veterinary medicinal product (VMP) is any substance or combination of substances presented as having properties for treating or preventing disease in animals, or any substance that may be used in or administered to animals to restore, correct or modify physiological functions by exerting a pharmacological, immunological or metabolic action, or making a medical diagnosis (Veterinary Medicines Regulations 2008).

KeyPoints

set out the classifications and circumstances for the sale or supply of each.

Prescription-only medicine – veterinarian (POM-V) and prescription-only medicine – veterinarian, pharmacist, suitably qualified person (POM-VPS) can only be supplied against a valid veterinary prescription. The main difference between these two classes is that a suitably qualified person (SQP), in addition to a veterinary surgeon or a pharmacist, can supply the VPS category. A SQP has trained and registered to be able to sell a limited range of veterinary products, often working in a pet shop, saddlery or agricultural merchant's premises. For both of these categories the prescription requirements are the same and a record must be made of the supply, and this record is then retained for a minimum of 5 years.

For the class of non-food-producing animal – veterinarian, pharmacist, suitably qualified person (NFA-VPS) medicines, no prescription is required and no records of receipt or supply need to be made, although it is considered good practice to do so. Sale or supply is restricted to veterinarians, pharmacists and SQPs.

Authorised veterinary medicines – General Sales List (AVM-GSL) have no restrictions on their sale.

Prescription requirements

The regulations set out the requirements for veterinary prescriptions (POM-V and POM-VPS). In the main, these are the same as the Medicines Act 1968 requirements for human medicines, with in addition the following items:

- the telephone number of the prescriber
- the name and address of the animal's keeper
- the address at which the animal is normally kept if this is not the owner's address
- the species of animal, its identification and, if a herd, the number of animals being treated
- the amount of product being prescribed
- the withdrawal period if relevant.

The withdrawal period is relevant in medicating food-producing animals, that is animals whose meat products may subsequently be used as food. Residues of medicines given to that animal may remain in the tissues for a considerable time. This will vary depending on the pharmacokinetics of the medicine in question but, to avoid any risk of secondary exposure to medicine though ingestion of such food, a withdrawal period is specified. The regulations set out the period of time that must elapse between the final dose being given and the slaughter of the animal. It is important to note that what is considered to be a food-producing animal may vary; for example, a chicken may be kept as a pet or for producing eggs or chicken meat.

Faxed or electronic prescriptions are not considered to be valid prescriptions for POM-V or POM-VPS medicines, although they can indicate that a prescription exists and under certain circumstances it may be acceptable to supply against this. These supplies may be made on the basis that safeguards exist to ensure the integrity of the original prescription, that it is indeed from an authorised source and signed by the appropriate prescriber and that it has only been forwarded to a single pharmacy to supply. In addition, arrangements must be in place to ensure that the actual prescription will be received within a short period of time. The prescription cannot be for a controlled drug.

VMPs are licensed medicines. In many cases the licence will be species- or indication-specific. It is important to be aware that VMPs that are safe to use in one species may not be safe in another or may not have undergone clinical trials for particular indications. Animal physiology and pharmacology can vary between species and the licensing process is expensive and time-consuming. For these reasons a licensed VMP may not always be available for use; in these cases a system has been developed to allow prioritisation of medicines to be given to maintain the safest possible situation for the animal being treated. The first and preferable option is to prescribe a medicine that is licensed for the indication for that particular species. Where no such licensed medicine exists, the next option is to prescribe a medicine licensed for that indication in another species. Only where this does not exist can a veterinary medicine licensed in another European Union country or a human medicine be prescribed. Finally, if no authorised animal or human medicine exists then a prescription can be written for an extemporaneous medicine to be supplied. Prescriptions written according to this prescribing cascade must state that the supply or administration is to be made 'under the cascade' and include these actual words. Medicines supplied under this system have additional labelling requirements (see below).

Tip

Human medicines, even when they are a pharmacy (P) medicine or on the General Sales List (GSL), must be prescribed on a valid prescription if they are being supplied for animal treatment and should be under the cascade system.

Controlled drugs as veterinary medicines

Where a veterinary prescription is written for a medicine that is also a scheduled drug under the Misuse of Drugs Act 1971 then the prescription must also meet any prescription requirements for that schedule. This means that prescriptions will have a 28-day validity, schedules 2 and 3 drugs are not repeatable, and a record will need to be made and retained in the controlled drug register in addition to the POM-V or POM-VPS record.

There is, however, no standard prescription form, nor does the prescription need to be forwarded to the National Health Service agency for monitoring purposes.

Record requirements

All purchases and supplies of veterinary medicines, with the exception of AVM-GSL category, are subject to the requirement to keep records that must be retained for a minimum period of 5 years. This requirement includes controlled drugs. The record can be in writing or electronic but must be durable and permanent. The details to be contained in the VMP record of purchases and supplies are:

- date of transaction
- identity of VMP, such as name, formulation
- batch number
- quantity
- name and address of supplier or recipient
- for prescriptions: the name and address of prescriber and a copy of the prescription.

Labelling

Unless the VMP is being prescribed under the cascade, and is in the manufacturer's original packaging, there is no legal requirement to label a dispensed veterinary medicine. However it is considered to be good professional practice to label with the following minimum information: the name and address of the pharmacy; the name and address of the animal's owner; and the date of dispensing. Where the medicine has been prescribed under the cascade (see above), the label must contain the following information in addition to that on the label of a medicine dispensed for a human:

- name of prescriber
- name and address of animal owner
- expiry date
- warnings for the user
- the words 'for animal treatment only'.

Sale of sheep dip

Sheep dip (legal classification POM-VPS) sales require additional safeguards over and above the prescription requirements when being supplied. They can only be supplied to persons who hold a certificate of competence in the safe use of sheep dips. The supplier must make a note of the certificate number and keep this for 3 years. If the sheep dip contains an organophosphorus compound there is an additional requirement to provide an A4 laminated instruction sheet along with two pairs of protective gloves.

Wholesale veterinary medicines from pharmacies

Wholesale supplies of veterinary medicines are allowed to be made by community pharmacies. If the value of veterinary medicines supplied by wholesale is more than a significant proportion of total veterinary medicine supplies then a wholesale dealer's licence is required (less than 5% in any one year is considered to be acceptable). Records must be made and retained for at least 3 years.

Professional competency requirements

As with all other aspects of pharmacy practice, the sale and supply of veterinary medicinal products are subject to professional competency. A pharmacist involved in this aspect of pharmacy has a professional duty to ensure that his or her knowledge, skills and performance are of a high quality and up to date. It is equally important to recognise the limits of that competence and practise only in areas within that competence (principle 5 of the Code of Ethics). If a pharmacist's work requires him or her to supply veterinary medicines then that pharmacist should ensure that he or she undertakes the necessary training to enable this to be done competently.

Self-assessment

1. How often are the Veterinary Medicines Regulations revoked and remade?

2. What date do the remade regulations commence?

3. What do the letters VMP stand for?

4. Define a VMP.

5. The Veterinary Medicines Regulations have replaced the Medicines Act 1968 categories of POM, P, PML and GSL with four specifically veterinary classes: POM-V, POM-VPS, NFA-VPS and AVM-GSL. Briefly describe the meaning of each of these abbreviations.

Tips

Animal medicines are covered by separate legislation (regulations) from those dealing with human medicines. Although often containing the same or similar ingredients, the licensed indications are often different.

Certain medicines may be contraindicated in specific species or account must be taken of their use in food-producing animals – pharmacies providing veterinary medicines must be aware of this and be prepared, and able, to take this into account.

Four categories of medicines are set out under the regulations.

Arrangements for the supply of medicines 'unlicensed' for animal use are clearly specified within the regulations and subject to supply only against a valid prescription.

Records must be made of purchases and supplies of VMPs as required by law and these records must be retained for 5 years.

6. List the requirements for a legally valid prescription for a POM for veterinary use.

7. Identify the records that must be made for any prescribed veterinary medicines dispensed and indicate any retention requirements.

8. Describe what is meant by the term 'prescribing cascade' and indicate the impact this has for the pharmacist.

9. Outline the labelling requirements for prescribed VMPs not under the cascade.

10. What is the maximum period of validity for a veterinary controlled drug prescription under the Misuse of Drugs Regulations 2001?

Further reading

Bishop Y. *The Veterinary Formulary*. London: Pharmaceutical Press, 2001.
Kayne SB, Jepson MH. *Veterinary Pharmacy*. London: Pharmaceutical Press, 2004.
Snell M (ed.) *Medicines Ethics and Practice: A Guide for Pharmacists and Pharmacy Technicians*, 33rd edn. London: Pharmaceutical Press, 2009.

chapter 4
Misuse of Drugs Act 1971

Overview

Upon completion of this chapter, you should be able to:

- describe the background leading to the introduction of the Misuse of Drugs Act 1971
- understand the key regulations made under the Act that relate to pharmacy practice
- understand and describe the arrangements for lawful purchase and supply of medicines classified as controlled drugs
- demonstrate knowledge of the legal requirements for the sale, supply and administration of controlled drug medicines
- demonstrate awareness of the term 'authorised person', and be able to discuss its implication in practice.

Background

The term 'controlled drug' is commonly used in the UK to define drugs that have the potential to be misused or abused. The term actually refers to the controls placed on the possession, sale, supply and administration of the medicine, and not the nature of use associated with the drug. Amongst the public generally there is a high level of social anxiety surrounding the use of these types of drug and a potential stigma with regard to patients using this class of medication. Many effective medicines, classified as controlled drugs, have a legitimate use as licensed medicines for the treatment of illness. However some have a potential for misuse because they are physically or psychologically addictive, they may have hallucinogenic properties or they enhance sporting performance.

Unfortunately, history has demonstrated that, despite their medical benefits, these types of drugs have a propensity for overuse and abuse. As a result legislation has been introduced at various times in the past to try to limit and control the dangers they pose. The most recent of these is the Misuse of Drugs Act 1971. Before 1868 there were no restrictions on who could supply medicines and drugs. Many popular medicinal products available in the 19th century contained opium or its derivatives. These included: Godfrey's cordial, which was marketed as a colic soother for babies, and overuse of this product was attributed as the direct cause of death in many young children; Dover's powders, marketed for gout; and, most famously, laudanum, which was promoted as a tonic and painkiller. Under The Pharmacy Act 1868 the sale and supply of listed medicines were restricted to pharmacies and for the first time purchase of opium products such as those described above was restricted to sale only from pharmacies.

In 1912 the first international opium convention took place in The Hague, Netherlands. This resulted in an international agreement to introduce more extensive systems of domestic controls over the availability of narcotic drugs. During the First World War cocaine use amongst soldiers, who had returned to London from the fighting in Europe, had concerned the government sufficiently to pass regulations to control its use. These regulations were introduced under the Defence of the Realm Act 1914 and it was at this point that the link between the Home Office and the control of medicines was established. The Home Secretary was given powers to enforce the legislation and appoint officials to inspect pharmacies. In 1917 these powers of inspection were extended to include police inspectors and other senior police officers.

In 1920 the first Dangerous Drugs Act was passed. This prohibited the import or export of products in the newly defined class of dangerous drugs without a licence and, more importantly, it created a criminal offence out of breaches of the act. The Act resulted in opium, cocaine, morphine and diamorphine being classified as 'dangerous drugs'. It also established powers of inspection not just of pharmacies but also the premises of manufacturers, wholesalers and distributors of dangerous drugs. The Dangerous Drugs Regulations 1921 were drawn up under this legislation, to enforce its provisions. These prevented anyone from producing, supplying or possessing dangerous drugs without a licence, the exception being medical practitioners, dentists and veterinary surgeons. They also introduced the requirement that dangerous drugs could only be dispensed against a written prescription as well as record-keeping requirements for pharmacists and doctors.

Subsequent legislation was passed to create the Dangerous Drugs Acts of 1951, 1964, 1965 and 1967, each with associated regulations, to replace and strengthen the previous legislation. By the late 1960s concern was growing about the continued growth of prescribing of dangerous drugs and apparently irresponsible prescribing of these to addicts; however it was not until 1971 that the legislation was significantly altered.

The Misuse of Drugs Act 1971 repealed all the previous Dangerous Drugs Acts and the Drugs (Prevention of Misuse) Act 1964; however many of the provisions of the previous legislation were re-enacted. This was introduced to legislate effectively the trade and use of controlled drugs and was intended to prevent the non-medicinal use of these drugs; in order to do this, the Act covers both medicinal drugs and those with no medical use.

Misuse of Drugs Regulations

Regulations made under the Act define and control legal possession and supply for medicinal use and licences are issued to allow legal manufacture and trade in controlled drugs. Unless following the regulations or holding a licence it is illegal to possess, manufacture, trade, supply or use controlled drugs. There are numerous regulations that relate to controlled drugs (see below for details of some of these), the main one being the Misuse of Drugs Regulations that set out the medicinal schedules for controlled drugs and allow their medicinal use. These schedules determine the controls placed on the prescribing and supply of controlled drugs.

The first of these regulations were made in 1973 and following numerous amendments they were replaced in 1985. These 1985 regulations were again subject to amendment and remained in place until they were repealed and rewritten as the Misuse of Drugs Regulations 2001, the main change being to introduce changes to the way benzodiazepine drugs were regulated. The 2001 regulations continue to be subject to amendment, such as the significant changes introduced in 2006 in response to the fourth report of the Shipman inquiry chaired by Dame Janet Smith (Smith 2004).

The Misuse of Drugs Regulations 2001 (as amended) stipulate how controlled drugs may be prescribed on prescription, how they are handled and stored in pharmacies and how they are supplied to patients. The schedules to the regulations determine how a pharmacist should progress in handling controlled drugs for supply to patients by prescription, patient group direction or over-the-counter sale.

There are five schedules to the Misuse of Drugs Regulations 2001, although only four of these are relevant to daily pharmacy practice. These are numbered schedules 1–5, with

KeyPoints

Brief outline of classes of controlled drugs

The Misuse of Drugs Act 1971 categorises controlled drugs into three distinct classes: A, B and C. The classes are not relevant to the authorised prescribing and supply of controlled drugs; the requirements relating to this are set out in the schedules in the regulations (see later).

Class A drugs are considered to be the most harmful. Examples include ecstasy, lysergic acid diethylamide (LSD), diamorphine (heroin), cocaine (powder or crack), magic mushrooms (mushrooms that contain psilocin or psilocin esters), methylamphetamine (crystal meth) and amphetamines for injection.

Class B drugs include cannabis, amphetamines, methylphenidate and pholcodine.

Class C drugs include tranquillisers, some painkillers, gamma-hydroxybutyrate (GHB) and ketamine.

The penalties for illegal possession and supply are very strict and vary according to the class of controlled drug.

Offences under the act include:

- unlawful possession of a controlled substance
- possession of a controlled substance with intent to supply
- supplying or offering to supply a controlled drug (with or without payment)
- unlawfully allowing premises that you occupy or manage to be used for the purpose of producing or supplying controlled drugs.

Class A drugs incur the highest penalties for illegal possession and supply, and class C the lowest. Illegal possession of a class C drug can result in being imprisoned for up to 2 years, and illegal supply for up to 14 years.

schedule 1 being subject to the most stringent controls and schedule 5 having the least restrictive controls.

Schedule 1 includes drugs with no medicinal uses. A Home Office licence is required for the manufacture, possession and supply of these. Pharmacists should have no involvement with these substances, with the exception of the unlicensed, named-patient-only product Sativex, until it receives licensing approval from the Medicines and Healthcare products Regulatory Authority, when it is expected to be classified as schedule 4. A pharmacist may potentially come into contact with schedule 1 controlled drugs when patients seek to dispose of cannabinoid-based products as a result of having taken part in a clinical trial, for example in the early stages of testing for Sativex. If this situation were to occur advice should be sought immediately from the professional regulatory body and the Home Office.

Schedule 2 controlled drugs include the medicinal opioids (e.g. morphine and diamorphine), medicinal stimulants and the more potent barbiturates that are associated with a greater likelihood of dependence. Drugs within this schedule have the highest level of restrictions for manufacture, possession and supply. Pharmacists are legally authorised to manufacture and supply schedule 2 controlled drugs. Although manufacture is no longer common in community pharmacy there are some pharmacists who still manufacture their own products, for example methadone mixture. They are also subject to the prescription-only medicine (POM) requirements of the Medicines Act 1968; however prescription requirements are more stringent than for those medicines classified as POMs but which are not scheduled controlled drugs.

Schedule 3 includes the controlled drugs that are considered to be less likely to be misused than those drugs in schedule 2. The requirements for supply of schedule 3 controlled drugs are similar to those in schedule 2 but are not quite so restrictive: one of the main differences is that there is no need for register entries to be made. The most commonly used schedule 3 drugs in community pharmacy are temazepam, phenobarbital and buprenorphine. Midazolam was reclassified as a schedule 3 controlled drug in 2007.

Schedule 4 is divided into two sections: part 1 contains the benzodiazepines, for example, diazepam and nitrazepam, and part 2 covers anabolic steroids for medicinal use. The restrictions on part 1 of the schedule are much

KeyPoints

Other than schedule 1, each of the schedules also has a descriptive name, although often this is used in its abbreviated form:
- schedule 2: controlled drug prescription-only medicine (CD POM)
- schedule 3: controlled drug no register prescription-only medicine (CD no reg POM)
- schedule 4, part 1: controlled drug benzodiazepine prescription-only medicine (CD benz POM)
- schedule 4, part 2: controlled drug anabolic steroid prescription-only medicine (CD anab POM)
- schedule 5: controlled drug invoice pharmacy (CD inv P) or controlled drug invoice prescription-only medicine (CD inv POM).

more relaxed than those for schedules 2 and 3 but can still cause potential problems for pharmacists. These will be detailed later. It is worth noting that the drug zolpidem (Stilnoct), the imidazopyridine hypnotic, is included in schedule 4 as it has benzodiazepine-like activity.

Schedule 5 includes products that contain controlled drugs from schedule 2 as an ingredient but at a much reduced strength. The most commonly used examples are morphine oral solution, kaolin and morphine mixture, codeine linctus and pholcodeine linctus. Many schedule 5 drugs can be purchased over the counter in pharmacies.

Possession and supply

It is normally unlawful for anyone to be in possession of or to supply controlled drugs in schedules 2, 3 and 4. Exceptions to this include when they have been lawfully prescribed for the person, an individual holding an appropriate Home Office licence or those persons belonging to a class, such as practitioners and pharmacists when acting in their professional capacity, as specified in the regulations.

Purchasing controlled drug stock

When a pharmacist purchases controlled drugs from wholesalers or manufacturers for stock the level of record keeping required will differ depending on the schedule to which the preparation belongs. For schedule 2 controlled drugs the legislation requires that all purchases must be recorded in a controlled drug register either on the date of receipt or by the end of the next following day. These records must be recorded in chronological order (in sequence according to time) and the minimum requirements for the controlled drug register, which may be maintained electronically or as a paper version, are set out in the regulations. The register must be kept for at least 2 years after the last entry recorded in it (5 years if relating to veterinary medicines). An example of such an entry can be seen in Figure 4.1.

> **KeyPoints**
>
> For schedule 2 controlled drugs the following information must be recorded in the controlled drug register:
> - the date the supply was received
> - the name and address of the supplier
> - the quantity received.

The purchase invoice must also be retained for 2 years or 5 years if the controlled drug is a veterinary medicinal product (see Chapter 3).

There is no requirement to keep written records of purchases of schedules 3, 4 and 5 controlled drugs in a controlled drug register. It is however a legal requirement to retain the invoices, as above.

Supplies of controlled drugs

Controlled drugs in schedules 2, 3 and 4 may be supplied against written requisitions or prescriptions. The requirements for each vary according to

Entry of schedule 2 controlled drug obtained

Drug _Morphine sulphate (MST)_   Form _Tablets_   Strength _10 mg_

Date supply received or date supplied	Quantity	Name and address from whom received	Name and address of person or firm supplied	Details of authority to possess – prescriber or licence holder's details	Person collecting schedule 2 controlled drug (patient/patient's representative/healthcare professional) and, if healthcare professional, name and address	Was proof of identity requested of patient/patient's representative? (yes/no)	Was proof of identity of person collecting provided? (yes/no)	Balance
14/7/2010	120	Chemdrug Ltd, Sometown						120

Entry for supply made

Drug _Morphine sulphate (MST)_   Form _Tablets_   Strength _10 mg_

Date supply received or date supplied	Quantity	Name and address from whom received	Name and address of person or firm supplied	Details of authority to possess – prescriber or licence holder's details	Person collecting schedule 2 controlled drug (patient/patient's representative/healthcare professional) and, if healthcare professional, name and address	Was proof of identity requested of patient/patient's representative? (yes/no)	Was proof of identity of person collecting provided? (yes/no)	Balance
14/7/2010	120	Chemdrug Ltd, Sometown						120
17/7/2010	56		Andrew Smith, 1 The Green, Anytown	Dr N E Body NHS 123456	Andrew Smith	yes	yes	64

Figure 4.1 Example of controlled drug register entries.

the schedule. The most stringent requirements relate to schedules 1 and 2 controlled drugs. For all controlled drugs to be supplied to patients, other than those in schedule 5 that are classified as a pharmacy medicine, a prescription will be required. In addition to the requirements of the Misuse of Drugs Act 1971 those of the Medicines Act 1968 relating to the supply of POMs must also be met.

Prescriptions for schedules 2 and 3 controlled drugs, other than those for animals, must be written either on a National Health Service (NHS) issued prescription form or on a standardised private prescription form usually obtained from the prescriber's primary care organisation – see below for details. Standardised requisition forms are also available although there is no legal requirement to use these so long as all the legal requirements for a requisition are met. Written requisitions should be obtained in advance when supplying controlled drugs to other pharmacies as well as authorised persons such as practitioners.

KeyPoints

A written requisition to supply must be received before a pharmacist delivers a schedule 2 or 3 controlled drug to an authorised recipient such as a doctor or dentist. It must contain the following:

- the recipient's name, address and profession or occupation
- the total quantity of the drug and the purpose for which it is required
- the recipient must sign it in his or her own handwriting, although the remainder of the requisition does not need to be handwritten.

The supplier must be reasonably satisfied that the signature and occupation are genuine.

Prescriptions and the dispensing process

The requirements for writing prescriptions differ depending on the schedule of the controlled drug. The most stringent requirements relate to those controlled drugs contained in schedule 2, although even these have been modified by recent amendments to the regulations.

Since November 2005 prescriptions for all scheduled controlled drugs can be either computer-generated or handwritten, with only the prescriber's signature having to be in his or her own handwriting. Before this date only those prescriptions for schedules 4 and 5 controlled drugs, or for temazepam, could be typed rather than handwritten.

These requirements are not always self-explanatory. What follows is a brief description or explanation of what is actually required or allowed under the prescription requirements.

The prescriber's address must be in the UK and this is usually pre-printed on NHS-issued prescription forms but may not be on standard private controlled drug prescription forms (see below for details about these).

According to Home Office interpretation of the regulations, the form or formulation of the drug being prescribed should consist of a minimum

KeyPoints

Prescriptions for schedules 2 and 3 drugs are subject to the following requirements and to be lawful must:

- be signed by the prescriber with his or her usual signature
- be dated
- be written in an indelible form
- specify the prescriber's address unless an NHS or local health authority prescription
- be on a standardised form if a private prescription, and contain the prescriber's identification number
- specify the patient's name and address
- specify the form and, where appropriate, the strength of the drug
- include the total quantity or number of dosage units to be supplied in both words and figures.

If a dental prescription it must contain the words 'For dental treatment only'. If an instalment prescription, the directions must specify the dose and instalment amount as well as the intervals between supplies.

of three letters, for example, 'cap' for capsule or 'tab' for tablet. Abbreviation to 'T' or 'C' is not considered acceptable.

The strength of the product should be included, although under the legislation the strength is required only 'where appropriate'. However with the exception of products such as Diconal, which is only available as a single form and strength, most controlled drugs are available in a variety of strengths and forms and invariably this will need to be specified in order to be able to dispense the prescription item.

The total quantity of drug or number of dosage units is required and this must be written in words and figures. For example, for a prescription calling for the supply of 60 tablets of methadone 5 mg the quantity can be written as 60 (sixty) tablets or, less usually, as 300 (three hundred) milligrams methadone.

The dose of drug needed should be specified, for example, 'one tablet to be taken three times a day'. The Home Office does not consider the words 'as directed' to be an acceptable dose, although it has indicated that 'one tablet to be taken as directed' is. A potentially negative effect of computer generation of prescriptions is that errors involving the dose can occur. For example, if the pharmacist spotted prescriptions presented in a pharmacy for transdermal patches with a dose instruction 'to apply', this would result in patients having to be referred back to the prescriber for amendment, potentially delaying the start of treatment.

The prescriber's normal signature must be written in indelible ink. If the prescriber is unknown to the pharmacist then the pharmacist should make all reasonable attempts to determine that the signature is genuine. There is no legal requirement for the prescriber's name to be added in addition to the signature, although this is commonly pre-printed on to many prescription forms.

Since July 2006 prescriptions for schedules 2, 3 and 4 drugs have been valid for only 28 days from the appropriate date. The appropriate date can either be the date that the prescription was written, or the date that the prescriber wishes the prescription to commence. The use of a start date on a prescription that differs from the date of writing is more common with instalment prescriptions where the prescriber writes batches of prescriptions for patients at one time (see below for details of instalment prescribing for controlled drugs).

When the whole amount of a controlled drug prescribed cannot be supplied at the time of dispensing and the pharmacy has to issue an owing slip for the remainder, the patient must be informed that he or she must collect the outstanding balance within 28 days of the appropriate date. Note that this is not always the same as within 28 days of dispensing. Patients not advised of this may well be disconcerted or upset at any refusal to supply their remainder supply. Prescriptions and 'owings' for schedule 5 drugs are valid for 6 months as they only have to meet the prescription requirements of the Medicines Act 1968.

For temazepam and schedules 4 and 5 controlled drugs there is no specific format for prescriptions over and above the normal prescription requirements for POMs under the Medicines Act 1968.

Whilst it not a legal requirement, it is strongly recommended as good practice for prescribers to write prescriptions for schedules 2, 3 and 4 controlled drugs for a period of 30 days' supply or less. This is to limit the amount of drugs supplied and to reduce the potential risk to patient safety. Prescribers will often write prescriptions for more than 30 days' treatment and in such cases it is legal for pharmacists to dispense them. However if a pharmacist believes the prescription to be inappropriate he or she should query this with the prescriber who should be able to justify the practice based on the patient's clinical need. In some instances, for example, adult mental health, it may be necessary for prescribers to prescribe more than 30 days' supply; in fact some primary care organisations have policies for this. Pharmacists can ask for copies of these policies to reduce the number of queries they might have to make to the prescriber.

It is a legal requirement that prescriptions and written requisitions for schedules 2 and 3 controlled drugs must be endorsed with the name and address of the pharmacy plus the date on the day of the supply being made to the patient. The Home Office has indicated that the pharmacy stamp, if it contains the full address of the pharmacy, can be used for this purpose. The supply date and not the date of dispensing is required; if instalments are made or a balance of supply is owed the date of each supply being made should be endorsed; whilst this may seem onerous it can assist pharmacists with an audit trail, if any problems occur.

By law records of schedule 2 controlled drugs obtained and supplied by a pharmacy have to be maintained in the controlled drug register. Since November 2005 it has been possible for pharmacists to keep electronic controlled drug registers and as electronic prescribing progresses and information technology solutions improve it is more likely that electronic registers will become the norm. Presently the majority of controlled drug registers continue to be paper-based records and are completed by hand. Recent amendments to the Misuse of Drugs Regulations 2001 have resulted in greater variation in the design and layout of controlled drug registers, particularly in community pharmacy, as many pharmacy

KeyPoints

Minimum information that legally needs to be recorded for an entry in a controlled drug register:

- the date of supply
- the name and address of the person (or firm) supplied
- the authority to possess, such as the prescriber or licence holder's details (most pharmacists record the doctor's name and their NHS prescriber identification number)
- the amount or quantity supplied
- the identity of the person who collected the medication. This is usually the patient or representative. If the person collecting the medication is a healthcare professional then the pharmacist should record that professional's name and address
- whether proof of identity was requested (a simple yes or no is all that needs to be recorded)
- whether proof of identity was provided (again, a simple yes or no is all that needs to be recorded).

Tips

If a mistake is made in a register, always mark the error with an asterisk. If more than one error is made per page then number the asterisks. The best place to explain the error should be in the margin of the register. Crossing out, correction fluid or overwriting errors should not be used as these may infer that you could be covering a mistake even when an error may be a genuine mistake.

A pharmacist is required by law to keep a register for a period of 2 years from the date of the last entry, or 5 years if relating to veterinary supplies.

chains have produced their own versions. Some registers record purchases and supplies on the same page whilst others continue to use the older format with separate pages for recording purchases and supplies. This older style will often not have a space for recording the running balance of a particular preparation, although this is not a problem as maintaining a running balance, whilst considered to be good practice, is not a legal requirement.

Regardless of the layout of the register, certain information must be recorded for the supply of schedule 2 drugs. As with purchases of controlled drugs (see above), in this schedule any record of supply should be written in chronological order on the date of supply or on the next following day.

It is not illegal to supply controlled drugs to patients, their representative or a healthcare professional without suitable identification; however if the pharmacist is not satisfied with the identity of the person collecting then the pharmacist can refuse to make the supply. Pharmacists have discretion whether or not to ask for identification. Where a patient is regularly prescribed controlled drugs and is known in the pharmacy the pharmacist will sometimes not ask for identification as he or she has a professional relationship with that patient. In this situation the pharmacist will write 'no' when recording whether identification was requested and provided and then clarify this by writing 'known to staff' or similar wording.

Many newer-style controlled drug registers have a column for recording the running balance. Although this is good practice and can assist greatly in relation to regular audits of controlled drug stock, completing this is not a legal requirement, although at some stage in the future it may become one. Most hospital pharmacy controlled drug registers have recorded this information for many years, although until recently it has not become usual in community pharmacy. See below for more details about running balances.

Destruction of controlled drugs

Controlled drug stock sometimes goes out of date and can no longer be supplied. When this occurs the stock should be separated from in-date stock to prevent it from being supplied inadvertently against a prescription until arrangements can be made for its destruction, to be witnessed by an authorised person. At this point of destruction an entry will need to be made into the controlled drug register to account for the stock destroyed. The entry will be authorised by the witness and the running balance, where this is used, revised to reflect the new balance. Until it is destroyed any out-of-date controlled drug stock is still subject to the safe custody requirements.

Examples of authorised witnesses include the professional regulatory body pharmacy inspectors, police controlled drugs liaison officers, and those persons appointed by the accountable officer at the local primary care organisation (see Chapter 5). As it can take some time to arrange for a witness to visit the pharmacy it is advisable to rotate stock constantly and not keep excessive amounts of controlled drugs in stock in order to reduce the likelihood of their going out of date.

A denaturing kit should be used when destroying controlled drugs so that the drug becomes irretrievable. All controlled drugs listed in schedules 1, 2, 3 and 4 (part 1) should be destroyed in this way; benzodiazepines should not just be put in the standard pharmaceutical waste bin. An authorised witness is a person or class of person appointed by the Secretary of State or by an accountable person and must have undertaken appropriate training.

Patients, or their representatives, often ask pharmacists to destroy and dispose of unwanted prescribed medicines. Pharmacies are currently able to accept patient-returned controlled drugs for destruction from individual residences and care homes that do not offer nursing care. They are not allowed to accept waste from nursing homes as this is classified as industrial waste. Nursing homes have to make their own waste disposal arrangements and should be signposted by the pharmacist to the appropriate local authority. Any returned drug that falls under the safe custody requirements should be kept separate from stock in the controlled drug cupboard; it is therefore advisable to destroy patient-returned controlled drugs as quickly as possible.

Tip

Follow the instructions provided with the denaturing kit being used – these can vary depending on the type used. For example, some require the addition of water to form a gel and then require 24 hours to denature any drug added to them. In these circumstances it is advisable to keep the used kit in the controlled drug cupboard until the gel sets before adding to the pharmaceutical waste bin. Other kits may have different instructions.

It is not a requirement of the Misuse of Drugs Regulations 2001 (as amended) to keep records of patient-returned medicines. However it is advisable to keep a record of schedule 2 patient returns, whether in any bound book or, preferably, in a patient-returned medication record book. (Many companies that supply controlled drug registers also print such a record book.) Patient returns must not be recorded in the controlled drug register; it would create errors in the running balance, and more importantly increases the risk that patient returns could be redispensed. When destroying patient-returned medication it would be advisable to have another pharmacist observe or, if not possible, another member of staff, for example a pharmacy technician; however currently this is not a legal requirement.

Private prescriptions

Since July 2006 in England and Scotland and January 2007 in Wales any private prescription for a schedule 2 or 3 drug to be dispensed in a community pharmacy must be written on a standardised prescription form. In England this is called an FP10PCD, in Scotland a PPCD(1) and in Wales a WP10PCD or WP10PCDSS. Once dispensed the pharmacy will keep a copy of the prescription for its own records but must submit the original to the NHS Business Services Authority (NHSBSA) in order to monitor controlled drug prescribing nationally in the wake of the actions of Dr Harold Shipman. This requirement, along with many other recent amendments to the Controlled Drug Regulations 2001, was made in the report of the Shipman inquiry.

In England and Wales this standardised controlled drug private prescription form is bright pink, whilst in Scotland it is a beige colour. Its layout is similar to a standard NHS prescription form, with a few notable exceptions. The private forms include a unique prescriber identification number so that prescribing can be tracked. The back of the forms does not contain the normal NHS prescription fee exemption boxes as the prescription items will have been paid for by the patient. Private controlled drug prescriptions should be dispensed in the same manner as any private prescription with the controlled drug register entry being made, including the prescriber identification number and name under authority to possess. It is usual to include a reference to the relevant entry in the pharmacy's private prescription register. The private prescription should be copied and the original sent for monitoring purposes to the NHSBSA at the end of the month. The copy should be retained in the pharmacy as good practice for 2 years, as is the case with other private prescriptions. Remember that veterinary controlled drug prescriptions are not required to be written on the standardised prescription form or forwarded to the NHS

for monitoring; however the records of supply must be kept for
5 years.

Instalment dispensing

Arrangements are often made for misusers to obtain daily or
instalment supplies of maintenance doses of controlled drugs,
particularly methadone and buprenorphine. In addition to the
requirement for the quantity to be present in both words and figures for
schedules 2 and 3 drugs, an instalment prescription must also contain an
instruction for the amount of drug to be taken at each dose. When
prescribing under such schemes a special NHS instalment prescription is
often used and supplies are limited to 14 days' treatment.

Instalment dates should always be followed to the letter unless there
is a specific direction otherwise. The Home Office has set out specific
wording to allow for missed collection days and collection for days that
the pharmacy would normally be shut. This instruction should be
written on to the prescription by the prescriber as set out in the guidance
so that it is unambiguous. In addition to instalment prescriptions
some drug misuse services together with the primary care organisation
provide a service where consumption of the daily dose is supervised at
the pharmacy premises. These are normally enhanced NHS services and
are negotiated locally.

Running balances

Whilst not currently a legal requirement, running
balances for controlled drugs are considered to be
best practice. Running balances are relatively
easy to control if checked regularly. Solid dosage
forms and individual dosing units such as
ampoules and powder sachets are relatively easy
to control whilst it is more difficult to keep an
accurate balance of liquids due to many
manufacturers adding an overage to their bottles.
As a result there appears to be more stock left than
is indicated in the running balance of the register.
When dispensing liquids, checking the balance
after finishing each bottle of liquid can help
reduce this discrepancy, although the running
balance for liquids will always be approximate.
Measuring each bottle of liquid controlled drug is
not recommended as spillage is a risk when
pouring out; if this were to occur then it would
need to be accounted for.

Tips

Running balances should be checked
regularly; this reduces the risk of error
and makes it easier to spot
discrepancies in a running balance.

When counting stock for a running
balance, write down a list of products
and how many units there are in
stock. If you check that the amount
matches the running balance before
you write, you reduce the risk of an
incorrect entry and can reconcile any
discrepancy before writing in the
register. Some pharmacists use a
pre-printed list of stock and record
the balances against this before
checking the register; this may make
the stock check easier and quicker to
count.

Tips

Register discrepancies

Discrepancies can occur and these are often picked up when auditing the running balance. If there are fewer units of drug in the controlled drug cupboard than in the register this could be for a number of possible reasons, which may include:

- a supply has not been entered
- an entry made under obtained or supplied may be incorrect
- stock may have been left out of the controlled drug cupboard
- an entry may have been made under a different strength by mistake
- a controlled drug may have been returned to the wholesaler and not recorded.

When there are more units of drug in the controlled drug cupboard than in the register the reasons may include:

- a supply may have been entered twice
- a purchase may not have been entered
- there may have been a calculation error in the register.

If there is an error in recording it may be advisable to contact the wholesalers as they should have a record of everything you have purchased.

KeyPoints

The primary legislation governing drugs likely to cause harm through addiction and misuse is the Misuse of Drugs Act 1971. This makes it a crime to possess or supply controlled drugs unlawfully and specifies the drugs into classes A, B and C in relation to enforcing the Act.

The main delegated legislation is the Misuse of Drugs Regulations

When carrying out a balance check there is no specific requirement for the form of record to the effect that a check has taken place. Many pharmacists sign and date the current running balance when they complete a check, with some producing and printing out their own spreadsheets to record their checks, using the spreadsheet as a reminder. Other pharmacists make a specific entry on a separate line of the register every time they complete a balance check and if there is a discrepancy they use this opportunity to record the discrepancy and how they have resolved it. Whilst this method has benefits, in registers where there is only space for 10 or fewer entries on each page this method may result in the register filling relatively quickly.

Other legislation

The Controlled Drug (Supervision of Management and Use) Regulations 2006 determine the function of accountable officers, their ability to inspect premises and the cooperation of organisations that have involvement with controlled drugs.

These regulations came into force at the beginning of 2007 and require pharmacists to have a standard operating procedure in place for maintaining records of schedule 2 patient-returned medication and its destruction. By default it is also a legal requirement to have up-to-date procedures in place for the receipt and destruction of other schedule 2 controlled drugs.

These regulations also introduced the requirement for pharmacies to make a return annually to the primary care organisation.

The Misuse of Drugs (Safe Custody) Regulations 1973 as amended determine which drugs require safe custody and set out how these drugs should be handled and stored when not in use. The storage requirements for controlled drugs vary depending on the schedule and the Safe Custody Regulations set out the type of cabinets suitable for storing controlled drugs within a pharmacy. Generally controlled drug cabinets should have a double-locking mechanism and should be bolted to the floor or wall with rag or wall bolts. Other storage facilities such as rooms or safes can be used but only if they meet the standard required by the regulations; a certificate of approval issued by the police must be obtained prior to use.

The safe custody requirements mean that pharmacists must keep controlled drugs in a locked cabinet when not currently in use – when they are not actually in the process of being dispensed. Access to controlled drugs must be restricted to the pharmacist or to members of staff authorised by the pharmacist, as set out in the standard operating procedures for the pharmacy.

Safe custody regulations apply to all schedule 2 controlled drugs, with the exception of quinalbarbitone. They do not apply to schedules 4 and 5, nor to most schedule 3 controlled drugs. The following is a list of the schedule 3 controlled drugs that are subject to the safe custody requirements: temazepam, flunitrazepam (Rohypnol), buprenorphine and diethylpropion (Tenuate and Tenuate Dospan) and midazolam.

2001 as amended which sets out how controlled drugs must be handled in relation to lawful possession and supply.

Regulations set out the details of record keeping and safe storage arrangements for controlled drugs, as well as for prescribing requirements and for destruction.

There have been many recent recommendations and changes made to the arrangements for purchase and supply of controlled drugs by healthcare professionals as a result of the publication of Dame Janet Smith's reports into the activities of Dr Shipman. Not all the recommendations have yet been implemented.

Self-assessment

1. The safe custody requirements do not apply to which of the following drugs?
a. morphine
b. midazolam
c. oxycodone
d. phenobarbital

2. The inspection of pharmacy premises by police officers with regard to dangerous drugs began in which year?
a. 1914
b. 1917
c. 1919
d. 1920

3. Which one of the following statements regarding controlled drug prescriptions is true?
a. Total quantity must be written in words and figures for schedule 2 drugs only
b. Veterinary surgeons must use an FP10PCD for prescribing controlled drugs
c. Prescriptions for controlled drugs are valid for 28 days
d. Prescriptions cannot request more than 30 days' supply of drug

4. **Which one of the following statements is false?**
a. Patient-returned controlled drugs can be destroyed by the pharmacist
b. Schedule 3 controlled drugs in stock that are out of date can be destroyed
c. Schedule 2 controlled drugs in stock must be destroyed by an authorised person
d. Patient-returned controlled drugs cannot be returned to the register even if unused

5. **Which of the following is acceptable when written on prescriptions of schedule 2 controlled drugs?**
a. 'T' for tablets
b. 'One as directed' for dose
c. 'Sixty' for quantity
d. 'As directed' for dose

6. **Which one of the following is not current legislation under the Misuse of Drugs Act 1971?**
a. Misuse of Drugs (Safe Custody) Regulations 1973
b. Misuse of Drugs Regulations 2001 as amended
c. Misuse of Drugs Regulations 2006 as amended
d. Controlled Drug (Management and Use) Regulations 2006

7. **Read the following pair of statements and indicate which of the answers a–d below is correct:**
i. A prescription for schedule 2 controlled drugs cannot legally be written for more than 30 days' clinical need.
ii. A prescription for schedule 2 controlled drugs must be dated and is only valid for 28 days from that date, or the specified instalment start date.
a. Statements i and ii are both true
b. Statement i is true, statement ii is false
c. Statement i is false, statement ii is true
d. Statements i and ii are both false

8. **Which one of the following is true in relation to a prescription for temazepam, a schedule 3 controlled drug?**
a. Repeat prescriptions are allowed
b. Emergency supplies are allowed
c. Technical amendments to an incomplete prescription are not allowed
d. A record of supply does not have to be made in the controlled drug register

9. **Which one of the following pairs of controlled drug schedules may need to be kept in a controlled drugs cabinet?**
a. Schedules 1 and 4
b. Schedules 2 and 5

c. Schedules 2 and 3
d. Schedules 3 and 4

10. Which one of the following statements is true?
a. A controlled drug register for schedule 2 controlled drugs must be kept for at least 2 years from the last entry and 7 years if this was a veterinary prescription
b. A controlled drug register for schedule 2 controlled drugs must be kept for at least 2 years from the last entry and 5 years if this was a veterinary prescription
c. A controlled drug register for schedule 2 controlled drugs must be kept for at least 3 years from the last entry and 5 years if this was a veterinary prescription
d. A controlled drug register for schedule 2 controlled drugs must be kept for at least 7 years from the last entry

Reference

Smith J. *The Shipman Inquiry: The Fourth Report: The Regulation of Controlled Drugs in the Community.* Command Paper Cm 6249. London: The Stationery Office, 2004.

Further reading

Changes to the controlled drugs register. *Law and Ethics Bulletin.* Available online at: www.rpsgb.org/pdfs/LEBchgcdreg.pdfs.
Department of Health. *Safer Management of Controlled Drugs: Changes to Record Keeping Requirements (for England Only).* London: Department of Health, 2008.
National Prescribing Centre controlled drugs resource. Available online at: http://www.npci.org.uk/cd/public/home_page.php.
Snell M (ed.) *Medicines Ethics and Practice: A Guide for Pharmacists and Pharmacy Technicians*, 32nd edn. London: Pharmaceutical Press, 2008.

chapter 5

Health Acts 1999 and 2006

Overview

Upon completion of this chapter, you should be able to:
- describe the impact of the Health Acts on the practice of pharmacy
- describe the Pharmacy and Pharmacy Technicians Order 2007 with particular reference to:
  - fitness to practise
  - disciplinary mechanisms and professional regulation
  - continuing professional development
- discuss the reasons for introducing the responsible pharmacist legislation.

Introduction

The Health Act 2006 hit the headlines as being about smokefree places and changing the age for the purchase of tobacco. However if people think that this Act is only about tobacco they would be wrong. In practice this Act was like a peg-board with lots of things – many of the changes to existing practices – being hung on it. It makes many far more widespread changes to services in the National Health Service (NHS), including pharmacy, than just preventing smoking in public places.

The Health Act 2006 consists of a number of parts and within each part there are chapters. Part 3 is titled Drugs, Medicines and Pharmacy and the chapters within this affect pharmacy practice and the role of pharmacists. These chapters contain new concepts and make changes to existing laws, for example changes to the Medicines Act 1968, and in so doing these will have a major impact on pharmacy. These include having an effect on the role of some pharmacists working in primary care organisations with regard to new roles relating to controlled drugs. They will also affect other practising pharmacists who are provided with a more explicit definition of what it means to be in personal control of registered pharmacy premises.

Accountable officer

Chapter 1 of Part 3 of the Health Act 2006 relates to the supervision, management and use of controlled drugs. It introduces the concept of the

Tip

Part 3 of the Health Act 2006 relating to Drugs, Medicines, and Pharmacies is the most relevant to pharmacy practice. This introduces the titles:
- accountable officer
- responsible pharmacist.

'accountable officer', which was part of the government's response to the fourth report of the Shipman Inquiry (HM government 2004).

Harold Shipman was a general practitioner who was accused of, and arrested for, killing his older patients by misusing controlled drugs. He died by hanging himself in his jail cell whilst awaiting trial. A subsequent public inquiry under the chairmanship of Dame Janet Smith produced a number of reports and made widespread recommendations to government on the safe and secure handling of medicines regulated under the Misuse of Drugs Act 1971 and its regulations (see Chapter 4 for details). Her report into the deaths caused at the hand of Shipman indicated that some 254 people had probably been killed throughout the course of his working life. The recommendations, with the aim of preventing patient deaths, included advice to government to set up systems to share information between agencies and take a systematic approach to the early detection of practitioners who might be misusing or abusing controlled drugs.

The Health Act places a requirement on specified organisations within the NHS to appoint an Accountable Officer for controlled drugs. The role of this person is to ensure the safe use of controlled drugs within his or her organisation. So for a primary care organisation the role will include responsibility for bodies contracted to it, including community pharmacies, NHS doctors' surgeries and non-contracted providers of services, usually private general medical services located in the primary care organisation. The role includes the setting-up and operation of systems for safe management and use of controlled drugs and monitoring and auditing the management and use of controlled drugs. It also involves training, monitoring and assessment of people involved in their management and use.

For the purposes of the Health Act 2006 management of controlled drugs includes 'storage, carriage, safe custody, prescribing, supply and administration of these medicines, and finally recovery and disposal of medicines that are no longer required'.

Additionally, accountable officers have powers to make inspections of premises and record, assess and investigate concerns about improper management of controlled drugs. This section of the 2006 Act outlines the powers of inspection, including the ability to access and copy records kept under the Misuse of Drugs Act 1971.

The 2006 Act also gives the government powers to introduce regulations to make various organisations cooperate to share information about controlled drugs and concerns with regard to improper, illegal or unlawful practices with controlled drugs across health and social care. This requirement has led to the development of local information networks being set up by the accountable officer as forums for local health and social care organisations to share intelligence with each other and with enforcement bodies such as the police and inspectors from the pharmacy regulator.

The aim of all of these changes to the system of inspection and monitoring of controlled drug supplies is to ensure that the problems could be identified sooner than had previously been the case. If someone like Dr Shipman was misusing controlled drugs in his or her practice this would be noticed and interventions made to remove that practitioner from professional practice.

Medicines and pharmacies

Part 3, Chapter 2 of the Health Act 2006 provides for powers to amend the Medicines Act 1968 in relation to supervision of sales of medicines in registered pharmacy premises. It also amends sections of the Medicines Act 1968 relating to personal control, replacing the term 'personal control' with 'responsible pharmacist', referring to both registered pharmacy premises and bodies corporate. (To learn more about the Medicines Act 1968, see Chapter 2.)

It also allows for alterations to the Medicines Act 1968 to change the terms 'personal control' and 'supervision' within pharmacy. It does this by giving Parliament powers to change the enforcement powers set out by the Medicines Act 1968 so that when The Medicines (Pharmacies) (Responsible Pharmacist) Regulations 2008 came into force on 1 October 2009 the pharmacy regulator was empowered to enforce the new provisions.

What does the new role of 'responsible pharmacist' mean in practice and for the practice of pharmacy? To understand what these changes to practice mean we need to understand the circumstances that triggered them and go back to the previous definitions and interpretation of personal control and supervision. Since the implementation of the Medicines Act 1968, every registered pharmacy premises has been required to have a pharmacist in 'personal control'. 'Personal control' is the legal term that has been replaced by the new term 'responsible pharmacist' by the amendment to the Medicines Act 1968 as brought about, or enacted, by the Health Act 2006.

This term 'personal control' meant that there had to be a pharmacist within each pharmacy who was responsible for the pharmacy's systems and practices to ensure safe sale and supply of medicines to patients and the public. If there was only one pharmacist working in the pharmacy then this pharmacist was deemed to be in personal control. If there was more than one pharmacist working in the pharmacy then one of the pharmacists was deemed to be in personal control and the others were working under that pharmacist's personal control. Why is this control important? It meant that in every registered pharmacy premises, even those pharmacy premises that were part of a body corporate and therefore had a superintendent pharmacist, there was an individual pharmacist responsible for the immediate running of each individual pharmacy.

Quite separately from this element of personal control there are regulations around the 'supervision' for the sale and supply of medicines. This includes the supply of medicines against a prescription, a written direction, a patient group direction or as a sale of over-the-counter medicines that classified as pharmacy (P) or General Sales List (GSL). Detail on supervision in the law was scant. However the Royal Pharmaceutical Society of Great Britain (RPSGB), in its professional guidance, had over the years made clear its views that the pharmacist had to be personally available to intervene in every sale or supply of a medicine whether in accordance with a prescription or as a sale of P medicines.

This presenteeism, or requirement for a pharmacist to be present in the pharmacy at all times, put pharmacists at variance from other professions where supervision meant overseeing systems and/or practices of groups of professionals rather than personal presence and involvement. For example, a supervisor of midwives is a senior midwife with professional managerial responsibility. However, a supervisor of midwives does not personally have to attend every birth or every clinic visit undertaken by every member of his or her team of midwives. Likewise, a consultant physician is accountable for the prescribing within his or her team but does not personally supervise the writing of every individual prescription or written direction by all the registrars and house officers within the team.

Supervision of GSL medicine sales had been treated differently by many pharmacists as this class of medicines can be sold from any lockable premises. Custom and practice in pharmacy had been that a lower level of supervision had been provided and many pharmacists and pharmacy owners had taken the view that this group of medicines might be sold to the public even when the pharmacist was absent. However, there was no legal precedent to support or prevent this practice, until in 2004 Lord Fraser of Carmyllie, then the Chairman of the RPSGB Statutory Committee and a high court judge, gave an opinion. This stated that there was a different expectation of the level of care in a pharmacy compared with other shops and, therefore, even the sale of GSL medicines should be under the direct supervision of a pharmacist. The result of this interpretation, along with that of the RPSGB, on supervision meant that pharmacists had to be present in the pharmacy for all GSL medicine sales as well as for the sale and supply of P and prescription-only medicines. This created a problem that would take some serious legal changes to resolve.

In order to effect a change so that patients purchasing GSL medicines from a pharmacy could do so in the same way as they purchase medicines from a corner shop or garage, there needed to be a change in both the law and the professional guidance. Both of these changes needed to be accompanied by a strong communication strategy if all the pharmacists whose practice was going to be affected by the changes were to have a clear understanding of what the terms mean.

However, this proved complicated as the two terms 'supervision' and 'personal control' are separate within the Medicines Act 1968 but had become so intrinsically linked, particularly in the minds of pharmacists and guidance from the profession, that changes needed to be made incrementally. To make these changes the Health Act 2006 has sections that amend the Medicines Act 1968 definition of personal control and replace it with responsible pharmacist. The Health Act 2006 also gave powers to government to make regulations to bring about the implementation of the responsible pharmacist requirements.

The Health Act 2006 also gave the government powers to change the sections about supervision in the Medicine Act 1968. To date this power has not been used but the Department of Health has indicated that there is an intention to do so once the responsible pharmacist legislation has been implemented.

Additionally, the Health Act 2006 amends the NHS Act 1977 in relation to the role of the pharmacist in the supply of NHS prescriptions.

The introduction of the responsible pharmacist legislation provides for greater quality assurance and safety of systems. This will enable the government (with the backing of the profession) to revisit the legal interpretation of supervision and hopefully make the pharmacy interpretation of supervision more akin to that in other professions.

These changes do not, and will not, allow pharmacy staff to perform clinical, legal or accuracy checks, or assemble or supply NHS prescriptions in the absence of a pharmacist. Separate legislation under the NHS Act 1977 in the NHS contractual framework requires the involvement of a pharmacist in the safe supply of NHS medicines to patients.

The Health Act 1999

The earlier Health Act, that of 1999, introduced powers regarding the regulation of pharmacists and pharmacy technicians. Section 60 of the Health Act 1999 provided government with the power to change the regulation of pharmacists and pharmacy technicians. These powers within pharmacy profession are now commonly referred to as a section 60 order. This order replaced the previous arrangements for the regulation of pharmacists that had been set out in the Pharmacy Act 1954. The new section 60 order legislation is known as the Pharmacy and Pharmacy Technicians Order 2007 and for the first time it introduced the establishment of a register for qualified pharmacy technicians.

The order set out the powers of the pharmacy regulator. It gave the then RPSGB continuing regulatory powers to hold the register of pharmaceutical chemists (pharmacists), to hold a voluntary register of pharmacy technicians, and to collect fees for those purposes. Initially the power to hold a register of pharmacy technicians was only for England and Wales but the order was subsequently amended to include Scotland. The order also gave the RPSGB powers to approve qualifications and to accredit premises and providers of education and training for pharmacists, pharmacy technicians and people from overseas who want to be registered as pharmacists or pharmacy technicians in Great Britain. It also required the register to indicate whether a registrant was practising or non-practising.

It also set out a framework for new fitness-to-practise mechanisms which had been developed by the RPSGB after considerable consultation to replace the disciplinary systems (see Chapter 8). Transitional arrangements were introduced so that disciplinary cases that had been commenced under the old statutory committee disciplinary framework could be continued to be heard and subject to the sanctions available under that system. The new fitness-to-practise mechanisms were supplemented by additional powers for the professional regulator. They required the regulator to set out the expected standards of conduct and practice and so gave greater authority to the RPSGB Code of Ethics; in addition the order introduced the requirement for mandatory recording of continuing professional development.

KeyPoints

The Health Act 2006 has had a considerable impact on the practice of pharmacy through enabling legislation to bring about the appointment of accountable officers and the responsible pharmacist role. It is likely to result in the introduction of further legislation that will affect pharmacy practice.

Moving forward in pharmacy regulation

The legal framework to move the regulation of pharmacy from the RPSGB to the General Pharmaceutical Council in 2010 is set out in Pharmacy and Pharmacy Technicians Order 2009. This order replaces the requirements for regulation of the pharmacy profession that were established by the Pharmacy and Pharmacy Technicians Order 2007.

The Health Act 1999, through the section 60 orders, brings about legislation that governs the way the professional regulator meets its obligations for safety and quality.

Both of the Health Acts are intricately bound up with other primary legislation, such as the NHS Act 1977, The Medicines Act 1968 and the Misuse of Drugs Act 1971. The Health Acts work to modify their implementation and bring up to date certain aspects.

Reference

HM government. *Safer Management of Controlled Drugs*. Cm 6434. London: The Stationery Office, London 2004.

Further reading

Medicines (Pharmacies) (Responsible Pharmacist) Regulations 2008. SI 2008/2789. London: HMSO.

The Draft Pharmacy Order 2009. SI 2009/. London: HMSO.

The Health Act 1999. (c.8) London: HMSO.

The Health Act 2006. (c.28) London: HMSO.

The Pharmacy and Pharmacy Technician Order 2007. SI 2007/289. London: HMSO.

Overview

Upon completion of this chapter, you should be able to:
- describe the background to the setting-up of the National Health Service (NHS)
- understand the history, aims and purpose of the NHS, particularly with regard to its impact on pharmacy practice
- outline how the NHS Act 1977 relates to pharmacy practice
- discuss the NHS (Pharmaceutical Services) Regulations
- describe the elements of the NHS pharmaceutical services contract.

History, aims and purpose of the NHS

Healthcare free at the point of delivery has not always been the right of every person born in the UK. It was only just over 60 years ago that such a privilege was given to all. The NHS started across the whole of the UK (England and Wales, Scotland and Northern Ireland) in July 1948. Although it was established at the same time throughout the UK there are in fact three separate health services – those for England and Wales, for Scotland and for Northern Ireland – each established by different pieces of legislation. This chapter will focus primarily on the NHS as it works in England and Wales with some reference to the differences in Scotland and Northern Ireland. Reference to the NHS will generally mean England and Wales, but if Scotland or Northern Ireland is meant these will be referred to as NHS Scotland or NHS NI.

In the early 20th century, the pharmacy was the place many people went for advice about their healthcare. These were the places where free advice was readily available from a healthcare professional, but the National Insurance Act of 1911 changed health provision for many – mostly men. With the introduction of this Act of Parliament, employed men earning less than £170 per annum became entitled to free medical care provided by doctors who were 'on the panel'. This meant the doctors were paid a retainer fee to see and treat men covered by the Act.

David Lloyd George, who was a Member of Parliament representing the people of Caernarfon Boroughs (in north Wales) and later UK Prime Minister, introduced the National Insurance Act in 1911. A lasting result of this was that every man covered by the Act had a card and envelope on which his medical records were recorded. These cards became know as 'Lloyd George records' and this style of notes remain in use today, almost 100 years later, in medical practices where paper records are still kept. This Act was fine if you were a man in work or if you were wealthy enough not to need the healthcare cover provided by the Act. However, for women and children, even if your husband was 'on the panel', you were not and your healthcare needs had to be paid for. The alternative would have been to attend a charitable hospital, clinic or charity dispensary.

In 1939 Britain went to war with Germany and this conflict escalated into what became the Second World War (1939–1945), and it could be expected that during this period the government of the day had better things to focus on than what would happen after the conflict ended. Such an assumption would be wrong. In 1941 William Beveridge (an economist) was commissioned to look into the welfare needs of the population. His initial remit was narrow but it expanded to cover all the aspects of welfare and to set up a new welfare state in the UK. His report, published in 1942, set the priorities for the new postwar order. His main focus was to slay the 'five giants', that he identified as idleness, sloth, sickness, want and ignorance. Setting up the NHS was the response to the 'giant' of sickness.

To find the funds to take this forward a system of compulsory insurance (now called National Insurance) was set in place, to be paid by every working person, and sometimes called 'the stamp'. By paying their National Insurance adults and their children were entitled to free healthcare and benefits if they were sick or unemployed. The National Insurance payments were collected from salaries or wages.

A few months after the end of the Second World War, in 1946, the new Labour government set about building a modern welfare state for the postwar society. Amongst these changes was the creation of a new NHS, free for all people, to treat everyone 'from the cradle to the grave'. Aneurin Bevan, Member of Parliament for Ebbw Vale in south Wales, was one of the forces driving forward this free healthcare system. He lobbied colleagues, both inside and outside his political party, as well as professionals, charitable organisations and others, in order to try and get everyone who was needed signed up to provide services in this new, and some thought risky, escapade. The Act of Parliament granted to instigate this new system in England and Wales was the NHS Act 1946 and pharmacy was there at the beginning. The Act established local executive committees to provide services and these committees were charged to:

> make ... arrangements for the supply of proper and sufficient drugs and medicines and prescribed appliances to all persons in the area ... and the services provided in accordance with the arrangements in this Act [will be] referred to as 'pharmaceutical services'.

After nearly 18 months of debate – mostly between politicians and the British Medical Association – the basic infrastructure of the NHS was in place. Hospitals, doctors, dentists, opticians and of course pharmacists and pharmacy owners were ready to provide services 'free at the point of delivery' for NHS patients. These services started on 5 July 1948.

Community pharmacy dispensing and tax collecting for the NHS

From the first day of the NHS many community pharmacy owners entered into a contractual arrangement to provide medicines free to NHS patients. The new contractual arrangement was all about the medicines and appliances supply function. The pre-NHS role of pharmacies as providers of advice to patients and the public was neither recognised nor remunerated. That's not to say pharmacists gave it up, but it was not part of the services they were contracted to provide to the NHS and this advisory role was one that would be largely unrecognised for the next 40 years.

In the early years NHS pharmaceutical services were all about dispensing. The numbers of prescriptions dispensed were large and continued to grow rapidly. The government was expecting pharmacies to dispense 70 million items a year at a cost of £30 million. However, by 1950, these estimated numbers were eclipsed. They continued to grow exponentially through the rest of the 20th century and into the new century. For example, in 2008–2009 more than 790 million items were dispensed in primary care (that means outside hospitals) in England and Wales, with millions more in Scotland and Northern Ireland. Not all of these items were dispensed in community pharmacy; dispensing doctors dispensed a relatively small percentage of the total number of prescriptions usually in rural areas.

Unfortunately the NHS idea of services 'free at the point of delivery' did not last in pharmacy as a tax was imposed in 1951 in the form of the prescription charge. Pharmacists had to collect this charge from patients who were required to pay it. In order to ensure that pharmacy contractors collected the charge they were required to submit a monthly return to the NHS prescription pricing division and the total amount collected from charge payers was deducted from contractors' monthly reimbursement for NHS services. In this way pharmacists were perceived as people who collected money for healthcare and even now anecdotally people will say that pharmacists are making money from these charges rather than in their actual role as a collector of taxes! The cost of the prescription charge increases annually as it is linked to the cost of the average items supplied. The charge/tax is levied per item rather than per prescription form. This means that a patient who has four items on a prescription form may pay four charges. This can prove expensive for patients and many have stated that they cannot afford this expense.

Fortunately most people are exempt from charges and it is only a small percentage of items that are paid for, as so many people are exempt. Some items are free for all patients irrespective of their circumstances – these include oral contraceptive pills. Some people by virtue of their age or their medical condition are also exempt from charges. For people who are not exempt but who need multiple items there is a 'season ticket' or prepayment certificate which people pay for either every 4 months or annually. The price of this prepayment certificate means that people who need two or more prescription items each month will save money by buying a certificate. This is the current situation in England. However in Wales prescription charges were scrapped in 2007, Northern Ireland aims to have no charges from April 2010 and in Scotland charges will cease at the end of March 2011. The Department of Health in England is undertaking a review of charges but there has been no commitment to remove charges for all patients.

How is the NHS managed?

The structure of the NHS has changed throughout its history. The roles and functions of the management structure have altered but many of the basics remain unchanged. The government department, the Department of Health, is responsible for getting money from the public funds via the Chancellor of the Exchequer to fund the NHS. The following is an outline of the arrangements in England only. Students wishing to check the arrangements for Scotland and Northern Ireland should check the relevant NHS websites. The arrangements for Wales are similar to those in England, although terminology may vary.

England as a country is artificially split into large regions and healthcare in these regional areas is overseen by a more local NHS organisation. These organisations are currently called strategic health authorities. There are currently 10 strategic health authorities. Each is split into smaller, more manageable areas where healthcare is organised into primary care (care outside hospitals) and secondary care, which is care provided by hospitals (for inpatients or as outpatients). The organisations that are considered to be secondary care are currently called trusts. These NHS trusts can be hospital trusts, mental health trusts or ambulance trusts. The care of patients outside hospital is purchased and managed by primary care organisations. In England these primary care organisations are primary care trusts (PCTs); in Wales and Scotland they are health boards. Primary care organisations have two principal roles – commissioning services for patients and providing services to patients.

Commissioning is the process of procuring services of high quality and at the best value for a local population. The local primary care organisations are responsible for the local arrangements for the four contractor professions: general practice medicine, dentistry, optometry and community pharmacy.

Alongside the organisations listed above are a few special health authorities that are renowned centres of excellence. Many of the special health authorities have a world-class reputation and yet they remain part of the NHS and treat people within the NHS. Examples of these special health authorities include the Hospital for Sick Children at Great Ormond Street in London and the Royal Marsden Hospital for the treatment of patients with cancer.

There have been many models for the management structure over the 60 years of the NHS. Most of the models have put the patient at the bottom of the picture or left out the patient entirely. The current model puts the patient at the centre as a full partner in healthcare decision-making.

Provision of NHS hospital pharmacy services

Hospital pharmacy departments are not part of the NHS pharmacy contractual arrangements. Indeed current guidance prevents hospital pharmacy departments from applying for or being awarded access to NHS pharmacy contract lists to provide services to primary care. Hospitals are not required to have pharmacies, nor do they need to register the premises from which they supply medicines to patients under their care. Why is this the case? Medicines ordered, supplied and administered within hospitals are done so under a section of the Medicines Act 1968 that covers the 'business of a hospital'. The Department of Health has provided guidance to the NHS on what is considered to be the business of a hospital. Where a hospital pharmacy department wants to be able to sell over-the-counter medicines to patients, visitors or staff then it has to apply to register its pharmacy premises. This does not however allow the department to dispense ordinary NHS prescriptions. For more details on registration of premises, see Chapter 8.

Professional stagnation: early years of the NHS

As seen above, the early years of community pharmacy in the NHS were all about dispensing. Community pharmacy practice did not change much during the period from 1948 through to the 1970s, although a few pioneering pharmacists did try to encourage their professional colleagues to take on a more clinical approach. There were some major changes to the profession and these changes may be considered to be drivers or spurs for the more recent developments in community pharmacy practice and increasing the professionalism of pharmacy. These changes included: pharmacy becoming a fully degree-level entry profession; the growth of multiply owned pharmacies; and the increasing numbers of women entering the profession.

NHS Act 1977

The legal basis of pharmacy contractors' relationship with the NHS was changed. The NHS Act 1977 repealed (that means cancelled and replaced) the NHS Act 1946 and to this day the 1977 Act remains the current legislation from which the NHS contractual framework for community pharmacy is based. This 1977 Act gave the Secretary of State for Health powers to negotiate with the recognised body for pharmacy to agree the terms of service under which community pharmacy supplies general pharmaceutical services (the legal term for the services pharmacy contractors provide) under the NHS. The terms of service became a legal framework under the NHS Act 1977 and formed the requirements for community pharmacist contractors who provide NHS pharmaceutical services. This is why pharmacy owners are referred to as contractors or working under a contractual framework or working under terms of services.

The terms of service cover the rules that govern how a pharmacy owner can apply to the NHS primary care organisation to provide services to patients under the NHS. These primary care organisations are currently the PCTs in England and health boards in Wales.

The terms of service set out the lists of services that must be proved by all pharmacies in the NHS, the essential services. They also set the framework for other services which may be provided by some pharmacies depending upon accreditation (advanced services) and/or local arrangements (enhanced services).

The terms of service set out the processes to be followed for change of ownership of a pharmacy. Since 2005 the terms of service have also covered the fitness to practise of the owner, or board of directors and superintendent pharmacist where the pharmacy is owned by a body corporate (see Chapter 2 for legal definitions of superintendent pharmacist and body corporate).

Also covered is the process for getting on to a local pharmacy list – this is the list of pharmacy contractors in a specific area – a PCT in England and the health board in Wales. Obtaining a contract to provide services to be paid for by the NHS is not as easy as just wanting to do it. As this book goes to press the mechanism for providing these services is about to change in a new Act of Parliament. This is the Health Act 2009.

An unexpected catalyst for change

In 1981 a Minister, Gerald Vaughan, stood up at the British Pharmaceutical Conference in Brighton and at the biggest annual gathering of pharmacists in Great Britain said that he could not see a future for community pharmacy. This was not only very insulting to his audience but it was in some people's opinion the catalyst for changes in pharmacy that led to modern community pharmacy practice.

Throughout the next 20 years key policy documents (see KeyPoints below) were published by the Nuffield Foundation, the Royal Pharmaceutical Society of Great Britain and the Department of Health, each with the aim of developing a sustainable, more clinically focused future for community pharmacy. These documents took community pharmacy forward, leading to local developments of new services and eventually a move away from profits on dispensed medicines and payments for dispensing. At the same time the number of prescriptions dispensed in community pharmacy had risen to 790 million items in 2008–2009. This rise in dispensing volume, accompanied by a reduction in payments and profit on dispensing, has led to greater competition between pharmacies to increase their prescription volume. To some extent this competition for prescription business has been further driven by the failure to develop new income from other NHS services which have proved patchy due to the nature of their introduction.

> ## KeyPoints
>
> **Key pharmacy policy documents**
> *Pharmacy* (Committee of Inquiry, 1986) a report of a Committee of Inquiry appointed by the Nuffield Foundation
> *Pharmaceutical Care: The Future for Community Pharmacy* (Anonymous, 1992)
> *Pharmacy in a new age* (Longley, 1996)
> *Pharmacy in the Future: Implementing the NHS Plan* (Department of Health, 2000)
> *Building a Safer NHS for Patients* (Department of Health, 2001)

Other services (sometimes called devolved or locally administered services) were introduced in the 1990s. These devolved services were delivered according to a national specification and to a nationally agreed payment system but they were commissioned (purchased) locally by a health authority depending upon local need. There were few devolved services; examples included services to care homes and needle exchange services. There may have been a small number of these services; however they were a positive indication to pharmacists, commissioners and other professionals as well as to patients that the government was willing to commission more than just dispensing from pharmacy contractors, and that pharmacists could provide more than just dispensing.

NHS (Pharmaceutical Services) Regulations 2005

The framework for the provision of pharmaceutical services to the NHS is set out in regulations made under the NHS Acts of 1977 and subsequently 2006. These govern how primary care organisations have to administer and organise pharmaceutical services and have three main purposes: (1) control of entry to the pharmacy list; (2) fitness-to-practise procedures; and (3) terms of service. Many other regulations and directions affecting pharmacy are made under the various NHS Acts; however they are not within the remit of this book.

Control of entry

This is a devolved matter and different regulations are made in each of the four countries of the UK. What follows is a description of the system in England; space does not permit the arrangements for each country to be set out here but they are available from the respective websites. Not every registered retail pharmacy business is entitled to obtain a contract to provide pharmaceutical services to the NHS. Until the mid-1980s all any

KeyPoints

KeyPoints

pharmacy owner had to do to be placed on the NHS pharmacy list was to put in an application to the local NHS authority. However since then restrictions have meant that only applications for pharmacies that met the necessary and desirable criteria were granted a contract. Since the middle of this decade these criteria were eased slightly and four exemptions were created. These allowed for new pharmacy contracts to be granted where they were open for at least 100 hours per week, internet pharmacies, one-stop primary care centres and designated out-of-town large shopping centres.

The current NHS contractual framework for pharmacy services

The framework for the NHS contract is covered by devolved legislation. This means that the separate countries that make up the UK are able to determine their own contractual arrangements for pharmaceutical services. This chapter will concentrate on the arrangements currently in place for England; however the KeyPoint boxes briefly introduce the situations in Scotland and Northern Ireland.

The NHS contractual framework for pharmacy services in England and Wales

The contractual framework is agreed on a national basis; however the contract itself is held locally. This means that the pharmacy is on the list of the primary care organisation covering the area in which the pharmacy is located and not on the list where the head office is based. Why is this important? Well, it means that some services remain local even though the company that owns the pharmacy is a national pharmacy company, such as Alliance Boots, Lloyds or a supermarket chain with in-store pharmacies such as Asda or Tesco. This also means that, for example, Nottingham PCT does not have to hold the contract for more than 2000 Alliance Boots pharmacies just because the head office of the company is based in its locality.

In 2003 negotiations began for a new pharmacy contract building on what had gone before such as practice allowances, devolved services and dispensing that had existed before. A number of organisations were involved in the negotiations. These were the Pharmaceutical Services Negotiating Committee (PSNC), the Department of Health and the NHS Employers Confederation (an organisation that represents the interests of the primary care organisations that commission pharmacy services). After a long negotiation process, a framework for the new contract was put out to a vote of contractors in 2004. The vote was overwhelmingly positive and following the necessary legal changes the terms of service for the new contractual framework were introduced in England and Wales from 1 April 2005.

The new contract, as it is still called, is made up of three tiers (levels) of services: essential services, advanced services and enhanced services.

The three levels of service provision are enshrined within the legal framework of the terms of service along with a lot of other information. This other information relating to pharmacy contractors includes the processes to be followed in order to:

- make an application for admission to the pharmacy list
- establish contracted hours (core hours and supplementary hours) of opening and change them
- change ownership of a pharmacy
- suspend a contract
- carry out remuneration and reimbursement
- relocate an existing pharmacy
- establish fitness to practise.

The next few pages will deal with the provision of pharmaceutical services under the NHS, looking firstly at the three tiers of the contract: the essential, advanced and enhanced services.

Tip

It is important to know which services pharmacies provide and under which tier of the contract each service is provided. Without this knowledge it will be difficult to understand how each service is commissioned and remunerated.

Essential services

There are seven essential services, numbered 1–6 and 8. There is no essential service number 7; although originally envisaged, this was dropped during the negotiation stages of the contract when it became part of the practice payment. All pharmacies in England and Wales have to provide the essential services. Payments for these have been agreed at national level and will be the same for any pharmacy providing these services everywhere in these countries. Service specifications outline what pharmacists should be doing for each service and are available from the PSNC website (www.psnc.org.uk/page/essential_services).

KeyPoints

Essential services
ES1: dispensing
ES2: repeat dispensing
ES3: disposal of unwanted medicines
ES4: public health
ES5: signposting
ES6: support for self-care
ES7: there is no ES7!
ES8: clinical governance.

A brief description of each of the seven essential services is set out here.

Dispensing

Dispensing is the supply of medicines to a patient in response to an NHS prescription written by an authorised prescriber. Authorised NHS prescribers include general practitioners, dentists, community nurse prescribers or one of the other non-medical prescribers prescribing as supplementary or independent prescribers. Some of these prescribers are only allowed to prescribe from a limited formulary or list of preparations, such as dentists and community nurse prescribers. Pharmacy contractors are required to supply medicines and those appliances, borderline substances and chemical reagents that may be prescribed on an NHS prescription form. They must supply the prescribed items with reasonable promptness unless it is clinically unsafe to do so. This last aspect is a significant advance on the previous contract. This had required supply irrespective of the appropriateness of the prescription. As a result pharmacy contractors had to balance their contractual obligation to supply a medicine or appliance to a patient against their professional ethical requirements to ensure that they served the best interest and care of the patient. This conflict of requirements has now been removed.

Contractors are obliged to ensure safe systems of working, including having written standard operating procedures covering the dispensing process and other clinical governance requirements (see below). Records must be kept of all supplies and also of clinically significant interventions.

The repeat dispensing service

With repeat dispensing, patients whose medical conditions are considered to be stable can be issued with a prescription that permits repeats of supply covering up to a maximum of 12 months' supply. The prescription is written on an FP10 prescription form called a repeat authorisation (Figure 6.1). This form is completed and signed by the prescriber as a normal FP10. It states how many repeats are permitted and is issued to the patient along with a supply of forms known as batch issue forms (Figure 6.2). These are numbered and contain the details of which products are to be supplied along with the name and address of the patient and prescriber. However these batch issue forms are not signed. The NHS FP10 forms are both a legal prescription for prescription-only medicine (and authorisation to supply pharmacy medications and General Sales List) and also an invoice for payment to allow the pharmacy contractor to be reimbursed by the NHS for the cost of the medicines/ appliance, along with remuneration of the associated NHS fees.

Patients have the convenience of receiving their medicines from the pharmacy when they need the products without having to visit the doctor for a prescription. They have the opportunity to speak with the pharmacist when they collect medicines and so can discuss any changes

Pharmacy stamp	Age	Title, forename, surname and address
	Date of birth	Must have: *Name of patient* *Address of patient*
Please don't stamp over age box		

Number of days' treatment N.B.: Ensure dose is stated	

Endorsements	**GP repeat dispensing** Authorising no. of issues = *Y*	*RA*

Signature of prescriber *Must be signed*	Date *Must be dated*

For dispenser: No. of prescriptions on form	**Dr N E Body** **888666** The Surgery 1 School Road Anytown 01234 567890	*RA*

NHS	Patients – please read the notes overleaf
	54365421321

Figure 6.1 Repeat authorisation (RA) form.

to their condition and/or any problems they are having with medicine usage.

This system differs significantly from, and should not be confused with, repeat prescribing services. The repeat prescribing service involves patients having to request a prescription from their GP surgery for

Pharmacy stamp	Age	Title, forename, surname and address
	Date of birth	*Name of patient* *Address of patient*
Please don't stamp over age box		

Number of days' treatment N.B. Ensure dose is stated	

Endorsements	GP repeat dispensing	*RD*

Signature of prescriber **Repeat dispensing** *X* **of** *Y* *Not signed*	Date	*X*

For dispenser: no. of prescriptions on form	**Dr N E Body** **888666** The Surgery 1 School Road Anytown 01234 567890	*RD*

NHS	Patients – please read the notes overleaf
	54365421321

Figure 6.2 Batch issue form. RD, repeat dispensing.

regularly used medicines and the doctors would then, normally without seeing the patient, produce a prescription usually on a monthly basis for dispensing at a local pharmacy.

Disposal of unwanted medicines

The disposal of unwanted medicines service is to ensure that medicines that are no longer required by members of the public can be returned to pharmacies and disposed of safely within the relevant legislation (see Chapter 7 for further details of legislation dealing with removal of waste). In this service, arrangements are made and paid for by the local NHS primary care organisation for the collection and removal of waste medicines from community pharmacies. The pharmacy contractor is required to accept medicines from patients or their carers, who reside in their own homes. The benefits of such a service include reducing the risk of child poisoning in the home and the minimisation of environmental risk by ensuring that medicines are disposed of safely and included in household waste.

Public health (lifestyle advice)

The idea behind this service is that pharmacists, more than any other healthcare professional, are likely to see the 'well patient' regularly. It is about trying to help people stay healthy and aims to raise awareness of particular health problems and how to avoid illness. Examples include assessment and monitoring cardiovascular risk and reducing exposure to cancer-causing agents through promoting campaigns to stop smoking or reduce excessive exposure to sun. Pharmacies are very accessible environments, generally not appointment-based services, so pharmacists have the opportunity to reach patient groups that other healthcare professionals find difficult. The contract requirement is to participate proactively in up to six such campaigns a year. Participation in these will involve giving advice and maybe having in-store displays with the provision of written information. There is no requirement to link these campaigns to others; however public health and health promotion research shows that coordinated campaigns and consistent messages are effective. To be most effective with this aspect of the contract pharmacy contractors should work with their local NHS public health departments.

Signposting

This service acknowledges that pharmacists make informal referrals to other heath and social care professionals in addition to services such as patient groups, charities and other support organisations. The referrals can be written but do not have to be. Primary care organisations are required to provide contact details of relevant services in the area. Many primary care organisations have done this in the form of developing a local signposting directory.

Self-care

This service acknowledges that pharmacists have a role in helping people care for themselves. It is about supporting and advising patients who have long-term conditions and helping people with the choice of over-the-counter medicines for their minor ailments. Contractors are also required to take referrals from NHS Direct. It is a financial contribution and recognition by the Department of Health for a service that pharmacists have provided since before the NHS began. The service is to help keep people with self-limiting illnesses away from other primary care services.

Clinical governance

Clinical governance is defined as:

> a framework through which NHS organisations are accountable for continually improving the quality of their services and safeguarding high standards of care by creating an environment in which excellence in clinical care will flourish (Department of Health 1999).

Community pharmacies are deemed to be NHS organisations for the purposes of clinical governance. This means that pharmacy contractors have to abide by the principles of clinical governance. This is one of the reasons why essential service 8 is clinical governance.

Clinical governance is about the quality of the service provided and about how to improve the quality of care. In the community pharmacy it includes elements of performance management through audit, clinical effectiveness, staff management including contracts, training and appraisal, continuing professional development, and handling complaints and compliments. Obtaining patients' views of services is a good way of learning about what needs to be improved and this essential service includes a community pharmacy patient questionnaire.

Safe systems are important and this includes having written standard operating procedures in place to outline the roles and responsibilities of every member of the pharmacy team when undertaking key roles such as dispensing. High-quality services are about managing risks – so an everyday task such as monitoring the temperature of the refrigerator where medicines are stored is part of clinical governance. More serious risks must also be considered and this

Tips

Records

- You cannot keep records of every intervention – you would not have enough time to run the pharmacy, provide pharmaceutical services and treat patients and the public.
- For dispensing, repeat dispensing, self-care, public health and signposting, keeping a record is advised where the intervention is deemed to be clinically significant.
- Guidance on what interventions are clinically significant has been given by the professional body.
- You should however record every error (including the ones that do not reach patients) so you can look for patterns of error and try to prevent recurrences.

includes recording and investigating errors, learning from them and reporting significant errors to the National Patient Safety Agency.

Payments and the Drug Tariff

Many of these essential services are paid for on a piecework basis, for example there is a dispensing fee for each item dispensed. The rest of these services are funded through the payment of a practice allowance. These payments are based on dispensing volume, that is, the number of prescription items dispensed by a contractor.

Detailed information on contractor reimbursement and remuneration is contained in the Drug Tariff that is published in hard copy on a monthly basis, although increasingly this is being replaced by an electronic version available on the internet. Reimbursement is the amount of money the contractor receives to cover the cost of purchasing the products – medicines, appliances, borderline substances or reagents, which are supplied against an NHS prescription. Remuneration is the money paid as the fees and allowances for services provided, some of which are based on the number of items dispensed. Other fees, such as the fees for medicines use reviews, are not linked to number of prescriptions. Remuneration that is agreed nationally, which includes payment for essential and advanced services, is detailed in the Drug Tariff. Payments for enhanced services are agreed locally between the local pharmaceutical committee and the primary care organisation and are not included in the Drug Tariff. The Drug Tariff is the legal declaration of the payment systems to pharmacy contractors in England and Wales for pharmaceutical services provided to the NHS.

There are both paper and electronic versions of the Drug Tariff available to pharmacy contractors. Both versions have sections on appliances, for example dressings, stockings, needles and syringes; borderline substances, including foods and cosmetics; and chemical reagents that are reimbursed by the NHS. It also includes the list of products and medicines which are 'blacklisted', which means they should not be prescribed on the NHS and pharmacy contractors who dispense these items will not receive payment for them.

The Drug Tariff also provides guidance on prescription charges and details on how to submit the contractors' monthly returns to the pricing authority so that they receive reimbursement and remuneration for the services provided.

> **Tip**
>
> Many people find the Drug Tariff a little scary or offputting due to the legalistic language. There is help available in the form of written or online resources from the National Pharmacy Association, the Pharmaceutical Services Negotiating Committee and the Prescription Pricing Authority. Courses are also available.

Advanced and enhanced services

The two remaining levels of the pharmacy contractual framework are called advanced and enhanced services. The legal framework that governs the contractual arrangements for advanced and enhanced pharmaceutical services is the secondary legislation, the Pharmaceutical Services (Advanced and Enhanced Services) Directions 2005. These directions have been subject to amendment in 2005, 2006 and 2007.

At the time of writing only medicines use review and the linked prescription intervention service are available to pharmacies under the advanced service level of the contract. To undertake these services both the pharmacist and the pharmacy need to be accredited. Accreditation for the pharmacist takes the form of a certificate awarded for successful completion of an appropriate training course. These courses are available from a number of providers, including the Centre for Pharmacy Postgraduate Education, some schools of pharmacy such as Reading, and as a collaboration between the *Chemist + Druggist* magazine and Medway School of Pharmacy, as in the Skills for the Future programme.

Accreditation of the pharmacy requires ensuring that a consultation room is available where both the pharmacist and the patient can sit down and have a conversation without being overheard. The contractor also has to make a declaration to the primary care organisation that the pharmacy premises in which medicines use reviews take place meet these requirements.

The medicines use review requires the pharmacist to review patients' understanding and ability to use their medicines. Its aim is to improve patient knowledge, concordance and use of medicines by finding solutions to the problems with taking medicines, improving clinical effectiveness and reducing wastage of prescribed medicines. The legislation sets out a number of requirements. This includes setting a maximum number of medicines use reviews per contracted pharmacy per year (currently 400) and requiring that a record is made on a nationally agreed template/form. It also sets out criteria for how often a patient may have a medicines use review and how any resulting recommendations are conveyed to both the patient and the patient's general practitioner if necessary.

Prescription-based interventions involve the same processes and paperwork as the medicines use review, but the starting point is different. It commences with any patient who comes into a pharmacy with a prescription and in the course of discussion with the patient the pharmacist realises that the patient has a problem with medicines and would benefit from a review of medicines taking. These are not subject to a maximum number per pharmacy per year.

The titles of the enhanced services in the directions are rather vague. This is an advantage for pharmacy contractors and for primary care organisations as it enables innovation and creativity in service development and commissioning. The directions are listed below, with some examples of enhanced services.

Enhanced services

- Anticoagulant Monitoring Service, where pharmacists test the patient's blood clotting time, including international normalised ratio, review the results and adjust or recommend the adjustment to the anticoagulant
- Care Home Service, where the pharmacist provides advice and support to residents and staff in care homes in relation to medicines ordering, storage, use and administration, recording and disposal
- Disease-specific Medicines Management Service, where pharmacists can advise on, support and monitor the treatment of patients with specified conditions, and refer patients to another healthcare professional as necessary
- Gluten-free Food Supply Service for the pharmacist to supply gluten-free foods to patients without the need for a prescription
- Home Delivery Service to pay pharmacists to deliver drugs and appliances to patients at their home
- Language Access Service, the underlying purpose of which is for the pharmacist to provide, either orally or in writing, advice and support to patients in a language understood by them in relation to their medicines and healthcare
- Medication Review Service, which is more indepth and more clinically focused than a medicines use review (an advanced service)
- Medicines Assessment and Compliance Support Service, for patients having problems with medicine taking
- Minor Ailment Scheme, where the underlying purpose is for the pharmacist to provide advice and support to eligible patients complaining of a minor ailment, and, where appropriate, to supply drugs to them for the treatment of the minor ailment at NHS expense
- Needle and Syringe Exchange Service, to drug misusers for the provision of clean equipment, reducing the risks of infection due to needle sharing and providing healthcare advice to drug misusers
- On-demand Availability of Specialist Drugs Service, which is useful for setting up schemes to improve access to medicines for palliative care
- Out-of-Hours Services, to permit pharmacists to be paid to dispense drugs and appliances in the out-of-hours period (whether or not for the whole of the out-of-hours period) when local pharmacies are closed
- Patient Group Direction Service, the underlying purpose of which is for the pharmacist to supply a prescription-only medicine to a patient under a patient group direction (see Chapter 2 on the Medicines Act 1968; this may include the supply of emergency hormonal contraception)

- Prescriber Support Service, to set up advisory services whereby community pharmacists can support healthcare professionals who are prescribers
- Schools Service, the underlying purpose of which is for the pharmacist to provide advice and support to children and staff in schools
- Screening Service: examples might include vascular risk assessment, *Chlamydia* testing, cholesterol monitoring or even pregnancy testing
- Stop Smoking Service, including voucher schemes, one-to-one support for people who wish to stop smoking and the supply of nicotine replacement products
- Supervised Administration Service: useful for supervised methadone and buprenorphine for drug misusers, but can also be used for directly observed tuberculosis services
- Supplementary Prescribing Service when the pharmacy has a pharmacist with the necessary qualifications.

Primary care organisations may only make payment for these services when appropriately trained and qualified persons working within relevant national guidelines or standards provide them. They must also have suitable premises and the appropriate or necessary equipment.

Contract monitoring

This outlines the role of the primary care organisation, the paperwork, the frequency of monitoring and the sanctions that can be applied if a serious problem is identified.

As part of the quality assurance of the new contractual framework, the primary care organisation is required to monitor the delivery of contracted services. This requirement is to demonstrate that the contractors are complying with the requirements of the contractual framework and to ensure that the large sums of public money are being used appropriately. This money comes from the National Insurance payments that all employed people pay.

A national organisation, Primary Care Contracting, in consultation with NHS and pharmacy bodies, led the development of a contract monitoring framework. This was done to help primary care organisations to undertake and set up the required monitoring and to inform community pharmacy contractors what the primary care organisations would be looking for in these processes. The monitoring tool is split into sections to cover each area of the contract and a copy is available from the Primary Care Contracting website (www.pcc.nhs.uk). Monitoring can be undertaken annually and it is important to note that the primary care organisation representatives have access to the pharmacy for contract monitoring purposes only. They do not have the right to see data about individual patients, so it is very important that contractors do not break patient confidentiality by allowing the sharing of patient data.

Pharmacy contractors (or the pharmacist working in the store on behalf of the contractor) are required to put together evidence to show that they have met the contract requirements. This evidence may be submitted to the primary care organisation prior to the visit. In some parts of the country both a pharmacist and a lay person undertake the monitoring visits. The lay person's role is to look at the pharmacy from the patient's perspective and to comment on the pharmacy service. The contract monitoring tool can be adapted for local use. Such adaptations need to be agreed between the primary care organisation and the local pharmaceutical committee, a group of local pharmacy representatives that is the official body with which the primary care organisation is required to discuss pharmacy services in a particular locality.

The monitoring is 'light touch', that is, it aims to find good things and to take a positive approach to improving the quality of services rather than being punitive or punishing poor practice. Where poor practice is identified the primary care organisation can alert the pharmacy contractor and give 3 months to improve. However the primary care organisation does have the ultimate sanction of withdrawing the pharmacy contract if the monitored performance remains very poor.

Fitness to practise

The details about the requirements for fitness to practise are set out in the terms of service; however the powers to require such declarations were set out in The Health and Social Care Act 2001. These powers apply to all four of the primary care contractor professions: general practitioners, dentists, optometrists and community pharmacy.

They allowed for all practitioners in these four groups to have to submit declarations of their fitness to practice; however for pharmacy these powers have so far only been applied to owners, directors and superintendents. There is scope in law to allow all pharmacists working as managers, employees or locums in contracted pharmacies in the NHS to make declarations. The Department of Health has been promising to extend this for some time and has even consulted on such a change. Many people within pharmacy have objected to extending the fitness to practise declaration to all pharmacists in community pharmacies within the NHS contractual framework. This is because most pharmacists working in community pharmacy are employees and, as such, are subject to appraisal and fitness to practise procedures within their contract of employment. Also, all pharmacists are subject to the fitness to practise and disciplinary procedures of the professional regulator (see Chapter 8 for details of the changes to regulation and to the disciplinary mechanisms).

The pharmacy terms of service outline how NHS fitness to practise is applied to pharmacy contractors. Currently, the written declarations of fitness to practise must be made to the primary care organisation. These declarations must include references about a pharmacist's competence and need to be kept up to date, so if the owner, one of the directors or superintendent changes then the details of the replacement, and a fitness to practise declaration, need to be made to the primary care organisation. For pharmacy chains each body corporate owning pharmacies has a 'home' primary care organisation to avoid having to make numerous declarations. For example, a large pharmacy company might have to make a declaration to each of the 150 PCTs in England and 22 local health boards in Wales. (The Welsh health boards were due to be replaced in October 2009 by eight local trusts and seven other bodies.) This home primary care organisation is the primary care organisation in which the head office of the body corporate is situated. The body corporate does not have to have a pharmacy with or without a NHS contract in the home primary care organisation. All declarations are made to the home primary care organisation, which will answer questions and give confirmation of fitness to practise if any other primary care organisation wants details. The home primary care organisation can also inform all of the other primary care organisations that have a pharmacy owned by the relevant company that there is a problem with fitness to practise with the owner, one of the directors or the superintendent of the body corporate.

Contractors in Scotland and Northern Ireland

The contractual frameworks in Scotland and Northern Ireland can be quite different from that for England and Wales, although many of the same services can be provided from community pharmacies. To find out more about the health service in Scotland and Northern Ireland, look up their respective websites (www.show.scot.nhs.uk and www.dhsspsni.gov.uk).

The future of the contract

In April 2008 a new White Paper on community pharmacy, *Pharmacy in England: Building on Strengths, Delivering the Future*, made it clear that pharmacy is a clinical profession and that community pharmacy will need to make further moves away from dispensing to develop its clinical potential more fully. The paper proposed a review of the contractual framework, in addition to making explicit the links between existing pharmacy services and national public health priorities.

KeyPoints

The NHS Act 1977 was tidied up by the NHS Act 2006 which consolidated earlier legislation and updated the language used. It did not change the law.

The NHS Act and its regulations allow for procedures for establishing a list of pharmacy contractors, fitness to practise and terms of service.

The Pharmacy Contract for England consists of three levels of service: advanced, enhanced and essential. Payment for services is determined by their level and can be locally arranged or national.

The Drug Tariff sets out payment details for essential services which are agreed nationally.

Self-assessment

1. **Community pharmacy contractors may dispense NHS prescriptions from three of the following groups of prescribers. Which prescriber is not permitted to prescribe NHS prescriptions?**
a. Pharmacist supplementary prescribers
b. General practitioners
c. Pharmacist independent prescribers
d. Private doctors

2. **Which of the following is an advanced service in the new pharmacy contract?**
a. Prescription-based interventions
b. Minor ailment scheme
c. Emergency supply
d. Signposting

3. **Which of the following is an essential service in the new pharmacy contract?**
a. Prescription-based interventions
b. Minor ailment scheme
c. Emergency supply
d. Signposting

4. **Medicines use review does not require which one of the following items?**
a. Permission of the patient's general practitioner to undertake a medicines use review
b. A standard nationally agreed reporting form
c. Pharmacist to be accredited to provide this service
d. An accredited pharmacy premises

5. **In 2008 the NHS was how old?**
a. 20 years
b. 40 years
c. 60 years
d. 80 years

6. **Which of the following is an advanced service in the NHS pharmacy contract?**
a. Medicines use review
b. Reviewing medicines usage
c. Medicines usage review
d. Review of medicine use

7. **The 2005 NHS pharmacy contract covers which sectors of the UK?**
a. Scotland and Northern Ireland
b. Scotland and England
c. England and Wales
d. England and Northern Ireland

8. **Which one of the following NHS organisations is not part of the NHS in England?**
a. Strategic health authorities
b. Special health authorities
c. Primary care trusts
d. Primary care groups

9. **The publication that sets out the details of remuneration and reimbursement of pharmacy contractors is called:**
a. Medicines Book
b. Drug Tariff
c. Medicines Tariff
d. Drug Book

10. **Which one of the following services is not provided by NHS contractors in England and Wales?**
a. General nurse services
b. General dental services
c. General medical services
d. General optometry services

References

Anonymous. *Pharmaceutical Care: The Future for Community Pharmacy*. London: Royal Pharmaceutical Society, 1992.
Committee of Inquiry. *Pharmacy: A Report to the Nuffield Foundation*. London: Nuffield Foundation, 1986.
Department of Health. *Clinical Governance. Quality in the New NHS*. HSC 1999/065. London: Department of Health, 1999.
Department of Health. *Pharmacy in the Future: Implementing the NHS Plan*. London: Department of Health, 2000.
Department of Health. *Building a Safer NHS for Patients*. London: Department of Health, 2001.
Department of Health. *Pharmacy in England – Building on Strengths, Delivering the Future*. London: Department of Health, 2008.
Longley M Pharmacy in a new age. *Pharm J* 1996; 256.

Further reading

Department of Health. *Drug Tariff*. Available online at: www.nhsbsa.nhs.uk/prescriptions.
NHS Community Pharmacy Contract Service Specifications. Available online at: www.psnc.org.uk.
PSNC Contract Workbook. Available online at: www.psnc.org.uk.

chapter 7

Other legislation relevant to pharmacy practice

Overview

Upon completion of this chapter, you should be able to describe and discuss the legislation in relation to the following aspects of pharmacy practice:

- dealing with disabilities
- holding sensitive and personal information
- health and safety at work
- destruction and removal of waste
- the sale and supply of poisons
- use and sale of alcohols and spirits.

Introduction

This chapter sets out a brief summary of some the additional legislation that may be encountered in pharmacy practice. It covers important information that pharmacists need to take note of if they do not wish to be subject to criminal action. Although not encountered every day in professional practice, it is vital that awareness is maintained so that situations can be dealt with effectively and professionally. There is a lot of other general legislation that affects the day-to-day practice of pharmacy; however, space does not permit it to be set out here. This chapter has therefore concentrated on the additional legislation that is most commonly encountered during day-to-day working in a pharmacy.

Disability Discrimination Acts 1995 and 2005

The 2005 Act was written to amend and extend the requirements of the Disability Discrimination Act 1995. Its implementation created new duties for all public authorities and required them to promote disability equality. The effects on pharmacy contractors of these changes were minimal. If a primary care organisation or other body contracts services to a pharmacy, then it is responsible for complying with the Disability

KeyPoints

Under the Disability Discrimination Act 1995 pharmacists are required to:

- treat disabled customers to the same standard of service as other customers
- make changes to the service provided to ensure there is no discrimination
- make changes to premises where reasonable to remove or reduce access problems so that disabled customers can use the services provided.

KeyPoints

The Disability Discrimination Act 1995 (www.opsi.gov.uk) section 21 states:

'Where a physical feature (for example, one arising from the design or construction of a building or the approach or access to premises) makes it impossible or unreasonably difficult for disabled persons to make use of such a service, it is the duty of the provider of that service to take such steps as it is reasonable, in all the circumstances of the case, for him to have to take in order to:
(a) remove the feature;
(b) alter it so that it no longer has that effect;
(c) provide a reasonable means of avoiding the feature; or
(d) provide a reasonable alternative method of making the service in question available to disabled persons.'

Discrimination Act 2005 by including this requirement to promote disability equality within the service specification. Any pharmacy that is contracted to supply a service will then need to comply to meet those terms. One change that did affect pharmacy was the change to the definition of mental impairment. Pharmacists can now include mental impairments in Disability Discrimination Act assessments if the impairment has a significant or long-term impact on daily activity. Before the 2005 Act, any impairment needed to be clinically recognised. By meeting the requirements of the 1995 Act pharmacists are deemed to meet their obligations.

For pharmacy the most important aspect of the disability discrimination legislation is section 21 of the 1995 Act (see KeyPoints). Its effect on pharmacists and pharmacies can be split into two sections: the pharmacy environment, and the supply of domiciliary compliance aids paid for within the pharmacy practice payments as part of the pharmacy contract.

Pharmacy environment

Under the 1995 Act anyone providing a service (for example, a retailer) must implement changes to comply with the duties set out in section 21 (d): 'provide a reasonable alternative method of making the service in question available to disabled persons'. Whilst it would appear straightforward to change the layout of a pharmacy to improve access for disabled customers, it may not be possible to anticipate every problem that could affect access for customers. Consider the issue of large and often heavy entrance doors that are difficult to open or steps up to them that might prevent wheelchair access. These problems would be expensive to alter and therefore more inventive solutions may be needed. Other problems that may hinder customer access and service include:

- There may not be enough space to move around the pharmacy.
- Lighting may be too dull or too bright and may affect partially sighted customers.

- Written displays and signage may be too small to view.
- Waiting areas may not be large enough or the seating may be inadequate.
- Shelving and counters may be too high to reach.
- There may not be a hearing loop for deaf customers.

Pharmacy staff, including pharmacists, should be well trained to support customer needs. They are required to listen to and act on any complaints or recommendations from customers. Most primary care organisations will review the access to services as part of their contract assessments and therefore pharmacists should actively seek to improve their premises where possible. However a key element of the legislation is that any steps that are required to be taken to accommodate disabled customers are reasonable in the circumstances. For example, if it is difficult for a wheelchair user to get into the pharmacy, the pharmacy may install a buzzer at the front entrance which can then be used by the customer to attract the staff's attention.

Domiciliary compliance aids

Under the current arrangements NHS pharmacy contractors are paid a practice payment which is calculated on the number of items dispensed each month. The payments include a fee for the provision of auxiliary or compliance aids to people who qualify under the Disability Discrimination Act 1995.

Such aids come in varying forms and may include:

- oral syringes, spoons and dosage cups
- tablet crushers and splitters
- grip devices for caps or winged caps for bottles
- tablet presses and punches for removing items from blister packs
- reminder and tick charts, medication alarms; multicompliance aids or clear and basic written instructions may be appropriate to assist patients with memory problems
- miscellaneous aids, such as inhaler aids, eyedrop dispensers, tube squeezers, talking labels.

Pharmacists have a duty to assess patients' needs for compliance aids under the Disability Discrimination Act 1995 and should not supply these without making an assessment. A resource kit containing assessment forms for pharmacists and for patient use is available from the NHS Primary Care Commissioning website (www.pcc.nhs.uk).

Records and confidentiality

Pharmacists have a duty of confidentiality to their patients, both legally and ethically. Pharmacists have to comply with the principles of the Code of Ethics that are supported and supplemented by professional standards and guidance documents issued by the professional

Key Points

Legislation governing confidentiality of information includes:
- Electronic Communications Act 2000
- Freedom of Information Act 2000
- Human Rights Act 1998
- Computer Misuse Act 1990
- Data Protection Act 1998

regulator (see Chapter 9). These documents clearly state the standard of practice expected of pharmacists. In addition to the professional standards, legislation is in place to protect the public; historically this legal protection was covered by the common-law duty of confidentiality. As record keeping and technology have improved, a number of legislative Acts of Parliament have been passed to control the use of data.

The Data Protection Act 1998 has the widest scope and the greatest relevance for pharmacists. It was passed to control the use of identifiable data stored on computers and replaced the 1984 Act of the same name. Its remit includes all identifiable data stored in any format, including computer files such as patient medication records; paper records like card files used for repeat dispensing; prescription forms and any receipts, dockets or 'owings slips' used in the processing of prescriptions. All pharmacies have to be registered with the Information Commissioners Office if they wish to process these types of data. The website (www.ico.gov.uk) includes an audit to determine whether an organisation complies with the principles of the Act.

Schedule 1 sets out eight key principles. These require permission to be requested before data can be stored; this permission should be obtained through a process of informed consent. An exception is when recording information is done in the best interests of the patient, for example patient medication records. This exemption is only valid on the provision that any information held is kept in the strictest confidence.

The information recorded should be up to date and accurate, with only the minimum amount of information such as name, address, date of birth, general practitioner's details and known medical conditions. In addition any information must be kept only for the minimum amount of time needed. Examples of this would be to remove any notes added to a patient's pharmacy medication record as soon as the information is no longer relevant or to change a patient's address in the record immediately the pharmacy is notified that a patient has moved.

Pharmacy staff must be trained about the requirements of the Data Protection Act 1998 and assessed to make sure that they carry out their duties within its principles.

In certain circumstances data can be disclosed to individuals other than the patient. This is unlikely to occur frequently but pharmacists should be aware of what can legally be disclosed and under what circumstances. This may include requests from other pharmacists and general practitioners in the interests of patient safety; police officers and NHS fraud investigators in support of serious criminal investigations; or judges and coroners in the process of justice and inquests. In the event of a court ordering information disclosure a pharmacist could be prosecuted for failing to disclose the requested information.

Special care is required when considering disclosure of information to a relative, parent or guardian. Personal patient information can only be disclosed with the consent of the person whose data is held. There is no minimum age limit to who can give consent: everyone who can understand the concept of confidentiality and their rights must consent for their personal information to be released to others. It should not be assumed that mentally disabled patients cannot choose whether to give consent and decisions regarding these patients should be made by the pharmacist on a case-by-case basis. Young children would not understand the concept of confidentiality and so it would be acceptable to share information with a parent or guardian. Teenagers however may understand this concept and would not wish for their personal information to be shared. There may be occasions when a pharmacist may feel it is in the interests of the patient to disclose information to a parent or guardian even though the patient may be able to give consent. Pharmacists should be aware that although they may feel this is ethically the right thing to do it is still in breach of the Data Protection Act 1998.

Tip

Receipts, dockets and 'owings slips' are often computer-generated and may contain sensitive data. The safest way to dispose of them is to shred them.

Health and Safety at Work etc. Act 1974

The duty of care of employers to their employees and users of the services provided from their premises is covered by the Health and Safety at Work Act etc. 1974 and the Management of Health and Safety at Work Regulations 1999. The Act and regulations have a wide scope and to cover them fully would require a whole book in itself. This section will cover some of the most important points of the legislation from the perspective of a practising community pharmacist.

Health and safety policy and information poster
Any pharmacy employing five or more members of staff must have a health and safety policy that should at least include the items covered in the headings listed below. The pharmacy should also display a health and safety poster (available from the Health and Safety Executive).

Pharmacies and other workplaces are subject to visits from Health and Safety inspectors and it is important that all staff are trained not only on policy, but also on how to use equipment safely and how to avoid or reduce risk.

Accident books/RIDDOR

Any accident that occurs on pharmacy premises, whether involving a customer or member of staff, must be recorded in an accident book. The entry must include information about whether first aid was administered or not. RIDDOR stands for Reporting of Injuries, Diseases and Dangerous Occurrences Regulations 1995. Under these regulations any serious accident must be reported by telephone as soon as possible to the incident contact centre at the Health and Safety Executive. A serious incident has been defined as follows: one that results in death, a customer requiring hospital treatment as a result of an accident, a member of staff sustaining a major injury or any dangerous occurrence. An injury that causes a member of staff to be unable to work or to be off work must be reported within 10 days.

Use of visual display units

All computer equipment and employees using these should be assessed to reduce the risk of injury as a result of their use. Implementing an assessment policy can reduce the risk of eye and wrist problems and lessen the employer's liability for any damage or harm caused.

Risk assessment

The point of risk assessment is to review the practices carried out in the pharmacy and to determine if there is a risk to staff and customers. Risks in a pharmacy may include: boxes that are a trip hazard, sharp-edged or glass shelving or the spillage of potentially harmful chemicals, such as bleach. The point of assessment is to remove the hazard if possible and if this is not practicable then to reduce the potential risk by changing procedures such as using protective equipment or storing products more securely.

Staff welfare

All pharmacy premises should have suitable facilities available for staff to use. This includes an area away from the shop floor for staff to have a break and where they are able to sit. Equipment such as a fridge and a kettle should be available for the preparation and storage of food and drink during rest breaks. Under no circumstances are staff food and drink allowed to be stored in the fridge that is used for medicine storage because of the risk of bacterial or mould contamination. Toilets should be provided for use and must also have hand-washing facilities with hot and cold running water for hygiene reasons.

Manual handling

Members of staff must be provided with training on how to lift and move heavy stock or equipment. This is vital to reduce the risk of injury to staff and to also reduce the risk of liability on the employer. If the movement of equipment or stock cannot be avoided then the use of equipment such as ladders, steps, trolleys or baskets may be necessary and this should be supplied where needed.

Personal safety and violence

Pharmacies sell and supply products that may be abused, for example, pain relief, laxatives, sleeping aids and high-value items such as razor blades. As a result there is a risk of theft and potentially violent behaviour from users of the pharmacy. Many pharmacies have an open layout and this can allow easy access to medicines and goods to potential thieves. The health and safety policy should include steps to minimise any risk to employees such as altering the layout or employing closed circuit television systems to improve vision throughout the store. Minimum staff levels may be specified.

Protecting the environment

The Environmental Protection Act 1990 set out the concept of duty of care in relation to disposal of waste. This means that the producer of waste is liable for the effects of that waste on the environment if not handled correctly through to the point until the waste is finally destroyed. The producer of the waste can be heavily fined or imprisoned for every breach of the conditions set out in the Act.

Since 1990 a number of regulations have been introduced to reinforce this legislation. In 2008 the Environmental Permitting (England and Wales) Regulations 2007 came into force, replacing the Waste Management Licensing Regulations, but left the majority of the regulations the same. These regulations require businesses that hold waste produced by another person or business to obtain a licence. The licence must be updated every year and is expensive. Fortunately for pharmacists there is an exemption to the regulations. This allows pharmacies to collect waste medicines providing the following measures are met:

- The waste is stored securely on the premises.
- The waste is not stored on the premises for more than 6 months.
- The total amount of waste received for storage should not exceed 5 cubic metres.
- The pharmacy must contact the Environment Agency to register its exemption.
- The waste is not classed as industrial waste.

The secure storage of waste medicines is classed as a simple exemption under paragraph 39(1) and does not require an environmental permit.

It should be noted that, as the pharmacist has a duty of care, the pharmacist should ensure that the person collecting the waste is authorised, the waste is disposed of at a proper waste disposal site and a consignment note is given to the waste collector. All consignment notes must be kept for 3 years.

Sharps waste is classed as clinical waste and not medicine waste under the Environmental Permitting (England and Wales) Regulations 2007 and pharmacies are not allowed to collect sharps waste unless taking part in a needle exchange scheme. Sharps waste collection is a local authority service and patients requiring this service should be signposted to their local civic centre. Pharmacies can however keep sharps and clinical waste for disposal, where this waste is produced in the pharmacy as part of a service; for example the clinical waste produced from services such as cholesterol testing.

If a pharmacy wishes to provide a service that involves the collection of waste from patients' homes as part of their usual business and customer service it must become a registered waste carrier and hold a waste carrier's licence obtained from the Environment Agency. An exception to this requirement exists where a pharmacy had an exemption under the old regulations, if this has been converted. In this case the pharmacy needs to take no action unless its circumstances change, for example change of ownership.

With the exception of those controlled drugs that are covered by the Misuse of Drugs (Safe Custody) Regulations 1973, pharmacy waste cannot be deblistered or denatured by the pharmacist as this is classed as waste treatment and requires a licence.

Waste returned from patients and residential care homes is classed as household waste under the Controlled Waste Regulations 1992. Collection of this by pharmacies for the purpose of disposal is covered in the essential services of the NHS pharmaceutical contract. However waste produced by nursing homes is classed as industrial waste and the nursing home must arrange its own waste collection contractors. Under the NHS (Pharmaceutical Services) Regulations 2005 pharmacies do not have to segregate waste, for example to separate aerosols, liquids and solids. In addition the Hazardous Waste Regulations 2005 as amended classified all medicines as not hazardous with the exception of cytoxic and cytostatic medicines. The definition of hazardous waste also includes single-use cameras, photographic solutions and shop lighting. Pharmacies only have to notify the Environment Agency that they are storing hazardous waste if they receive more than 500 kg of hazardous waste per year. Pharmacists should make attempts to identify and separate hazardous waste from non-hazardous waste where possible and it is an offence under these regulations to place normal waste in the hazardous waste bin and vice versa.

Poisons legislation

The supply of poisons to the general public from pharmacies is controlled by the Poisons Act 1972. If a chemical or substance is toxic but is not listed as a poison or non-medicinal poison then it is considered only to be a chemical.

The poisons list consists of two parts: parts I and II. Sales of a part I poison can only take place in a pharmacy and must be dealt with either by the pharmacist or under the pharmacist's supervision. Part II poisons can be sold from a pharmacy without the need for supervision or from the premises of a listed seller. Local authorities (local councils) keep lists of retailers who are able to sell part II poisons from their premises; these retailers are called listed sellers and they can only sell poisons under certain conditions. Many different types of retailers, from national grocery, do-it-yourself or homeware chains to local independent retailers, are listed sellers. Common examples of part II poisons include proprietary rat bait boxes, weedkillers and insect powders and sprays.

In addition to the two-part list, The Poisons Rules 1982 (as amended) determine how the Poisons Act 1972 is applied. The Rules consists of eight schedules into which the poisons are allocated and which determine how the item is distributed. Two of the schedules have specific relevance to pharmacy practice. These are set out in the following sections.

Schedule 1

Poisons listed under schedule 1 will also appear in part I or part II of The Poisons Act. They have special restrictions which include the pharmacist having to know the buyer prior to purchase, supervision of sales and supplies, requirements for signed orders and record keeping as well as storage requirements.

To supply a schedule 1 part I poison, the pharmacist must know the purchaser. If this requirement cannot be met then a householder can vouch for the purchaser's character by completing a householder's certificate that then has to be countersigned by a police officer.

Sales must be recorded in a poisons register. This is similar in format to a controlled drugs register, with two important differences. Firstly the pharmacist does not have to keep records of the purchase of the poison; the pharmacist only needs to record the supply. Secondly the purchaser has to sign the register at the time of purchase. The poisons register has to be retained by the pharmacy for 2 years after the last entry was recorded. Ideally the poisons register should always be kept in the pharmacy so that it is available for inspection; however this is not a legal requirement of the Poisons Act 1972. Many pharmacists keep their poisons register at the back of their controlled drugs register to stop it from getting lost. Anyone who acts as a third party to collect poisons should not sign the register as he or she is not the actual purchaser of the poison. In this situation a signed order can be used. If this is accepted it should be recorded instead of the purchaser's signature and a reference number should be given to the order.

Schedule 12

This lists poisons which are subject to additional controls because of the significant danger to health and the environment that they pose. Examples include strychnine and fluoroacetic acid.
Pharmacists need to be aware of these products as they may be called on to supply them in the event of a national emergency. However it is unlikely that the majority of pharmacists will experience supplying these products. Since 2006 pharmacists have not been allowed to supply strychnine and so the sale and supply of poisons from pharmacies have steadily decreased.

Poisons also have to comply with the Chemicals (Hazard Information and Packaging) Regulations 2002 as amended (CHIP) and must be labelled accordingly in English. CHIP symbols required on labels are usually square and in black on an orange background.

Pharmacists should be aware of the risks associated with poisons and should consider the Control of Substances Hazardous to Health Regulations 2002 (COSHH). For pharmacists it should be relatively straightforward to determine whether COSHH is relevant or not. Check the labelling on the package of the poison: if it contains any risk phrases or warnings then it is highly likely that a COSHH assessment will need to be completed.

Tips

Poisons should be stored away from food and out of the reach of customers.

They should not be stored in the controlled drugs cupboard as they could be accidentally dispensed.

Pharmacists usually keep poisons locked away in a cupboard or drawer reserved specifically for poisons to reduce the risk of accident or loss.

Alcohols and spirits

The use and supply of alcohols not for human consumption are regulated in the UK by the Denatured Alcohol Regulations 2006. In the past alcohol was commonly used and supplied from pharmacies; however with the increased use of specials manufacturers and the resultant reduction in extemporaneous dispensing, its use has decreased. It remains important for pharmacists to be aware of the types of alcohol available and the regulations regarding their sale and supply. Three main categories of alcohol may still be employed or supplied in pharmacy:

1. completely denatured alcohol, which was formerly known as mineralised methylated spirits, or by the more commonly used term 'meths'
2. industrial denatured alcohol (IDA), formerly known as industrial methylated spirits, is the grade of alcohol that pharmacists used when making external extemporaneous preparations
3. trade-specific denatured alcohol: this type of alcohol is unlikely to be used in pharmacy as it is most commonly used in the manufacture of propellants, toiletries, inks, cosmetics, screen wash, disinfectants and cleaning products.

Completely denatured alcohol

Completely denatured alcohol is usually purple and is poisonous if ingested. Sales are not restricted to pharmacy and it can be bought from most retailers as a cleaning or household product. It has to be labelled with CHIP symbols and phrases. The responsibility for ensuring that the label contains the appropriate information lies with the retailer; however in practice the manufacturer or wholesaler will have labelled the product adequately in advance.

Industrial denatured alcohol

Pharmacies need to obtain an authorisation from Her Majesty's Revenue and Customs in order to be able to purchase IDA. Unless a pharmacy has this, a wholesaler will not supply IDA. Pharmacists usually send a copy of their authorisation to their wholesaler every year if they wish to continue purchasing IDA regularly. Medical and veterinary practitioners can request IDA on either a prescription or a written order for professional use. They do not need to provide their authorisation certificate to make a purchase and pharmacists can supply without having to

KeyPoints

There is a large amount of miscellaneous legislation relevant to the practice of pharmacy. The following are of particular importance to the practice of pharmacy:

The Disability Discrimination Acts of 1995 and 2005 require reasonable steps to be taken to ensure that disabled customers and patients are able to access services provided by pharmacists and for needs assessment to be undertaken when dispensing to ensure that disability aids are supplied as needed.

All personal information held in the pharmacy about patients and other customers is subject to the laws of data protection and confidentiality.

The Health and Safety at Work etc. Act 1974 requires that workplaces have a policy and display a poster. Workplaces can be inspected to ensure compliance.

Waste produced by the pharmacy or collected there has to be handled in accordance with legislation relating with environment protection.

Very few poisons are sold through pharmacies. Poisons are classified as medicinal and non-medicinal poisons and the legislation divides these into two lists: part I, which can only be sold through pharmacy and part II, which can also be sold through listed sellers. The schedule determines the conditions for sale.

Alcohol is rarely used by pharmacies; however when industrial denatured alcohol, otherwise called industrial methylated spirits, is supplied, then the pharmacy must hold the relevant authorisation.

Tips

Large stocks of alcohols should be stored out of public areas of the pharmacy to reduce risk to patients.

All alcohol-based products should be kept in a locked cabinet; in pharmacies this is usually in a flammables cupboard. (Cupboards designed for this purpose are usually wall-mounted and bright red.)

Pharmacists stocking alcohols should identify where and how they are to be stored on any building plans. In the event of a fire, knowing their location will assist the fire brigade to locate the stock, contain surrounding fires, reduce the risk of ignition and harm to staff and the public.

check for authorisation, provided that the IDA being supplied is for medical use only. Records of any sales of IDA made following the receipt of a written order from a medical or veterinary practitioner will need to be kept. These should be recorded in the prescription register. Pharmacists do not have to make records of IDA being used to prepare prescriptions, unless the prescription was written privately.

Self-assessment

1. **Which of the following is not a stage of the risk assessment process?**
   a. Identify the hazards
   b. Decide who might be harmed and how
   c. Evaluate the risks and decide on precautions
   d. Discuss your findings with another person

2. **Which one of the following statements regarding alcohols is true?**
   a. Completely denatured alcohol is usually colourless
   b. Industrial denatured alcohol (IDA) can be sold in any quantity
   c. Use of IDA for extemporaneous dispensing of NHS prescriptions does not have to be recorded for excise duty purposes
   d. Trade-specific denatured alcohol is used in preparing medicines extemporaneously

3. **Poisons have to be labelled with safety symbols as laid out in which one of the following regulations?**
   a. CHIP
   b. HASAWA
   c. RIDDOR
   d. COSHH

4. **Which one of the following statements regarding poisons is false?**
   a. Pharmacists have not been able to supply strychnine since 2006
   b. Schedule 12 lists poisons with additional restrictions because of their risk to health
   c. Part I poisons may be sold by pharmacists and listed sellers
   d. Part II poisons can be sold by anyone on the local authority list

5. **Which one of the following is not a requirement of the Environmental Permitting (England and Wales) Regulations 2007?**
   a. Pharmacies must notify the Environment Agency of their exemption
   b. Pharmacies can store hazardous waste for up to 12 months

c. Pharmacies can store a maximum of 5 cubic metres of waste on the premises
d. The waste must be stored securely

6. **With regard to patient medication waste, which one of the following statements is true?**
a. Pharmacies can accept waste from nursing and residential care homes
b. Pharmacies can accept sharps waste
c. Under hazardous waste regulations pharmacies can accept up to 500 kg of hazardous waste per year
d. Pharmacists do not need a licence to collect waste from patients' homes

7. **Which one of the following is true under the Health and Safety at Work Act and associated regulations?**
a. Pharmacies do not need to display a safety poster if they have fewer than 10 staff
b. Serious accidents that result in hospitalisation or death have to be reported within 48 hours
c. Pharmacies must have a health and safety policy
d. Pharmacies do not legally have to provide basic health and safety training

8. **Under the Data Protection Act 1998 you cannot provide confidential patient information to which one of the following people?**
a. Coroner
b. Police officer who makes a verbal request
c. Parent of a baby
d. Parent of a teenager who has given consent

9. **Which one of the following patients would you consider for a compliance aid?**
a. A patient with memory problems
b. A patient with reduced vision
c. A patient taking multiple medicines
d. A patent with osteoarthritis in the hands and wrists

10. **Under the Disability Discrimination Act 1995, which one of the following are pharmacists not required to comply with?**
a. To treat disabled customers to the same service as other customers
b. To make major physical changes to premises to allow disabled access
c. To make changes to service provision to ensure no discrimination
d. To make reasonable changes to premises to allow disabled customers to use services

Further reading

Department of Health. NHS Information Governance – Guidance on Legal and
   Professional Obligations. London: Department of Health, 2007.
NHS Information Governance (Guidance on Legal and Professional Obligations).
RPSGB. *Poisons*. Legal and Ethical Advisory Service fact sheet 11. London: RPSGB,
   2008.
Snell M (ed.) *Medicines Ethics and Practice: A Guide for Pharmacists and Pharmacy
   Technicians*, 33rd edn. London: Pharmaceutical Press, 2009.
The Poisons Rules 1982. SI 1882/218. London: HMSO.

chapter 8

Professional registration and regulation

Overview

Upon completion of this chapter, you should be able to understand the reasons for regulation of the profession of pharmacy and be able to demonstrate knowledge of the following:

- the background and historical perspective of the profession
- restricted titles
- the role of the General Pharmaceutical Council
- the professional representative body
- professional accountability and responsibility
- fitness to practise procedures and outcomes.

Introduction

The profession of pharmacy as we currently understand it was established in 1841 when Jacob Bell and a group of fellow London practitioners set up the first Pharmaceutical Society of Great Britain. Its objectives were: to benefit the public; to introduce a scheme of education for pharmacists; and to protect the interests of practising pharmacists. Only 2 years after inception, the Pharmaceutical Society was granted a Royal Charter of Incorporation by Queen Victoria, thus giving official recognition to its role. It was to be 145 years later, in 1988, that Queen Elizabeth II conferred the title Royal to change the Society's name to the Royal Pharmaceutical Society of Great Britain (RPSGB).

The first legal register for pharmacists was set up under the Pharmacy Act 1852 and was restricted to pharmacists who had passed the Society's exams. This did not restrict the practice of pharmacy: non-registered chemists and druggists were allowed to continue in their business. Further legislation, the Pharmacy Act 1868, required registration in relation to the sale of poisons and set up the class of chemists and druggists as persons who had passed the Society's minor examination. By 1898, legislation changes allowed chemists and druggists to become full members of the Society.

Early in the 20th century, the Poisons and Pharmacy Act 1908 extended the title 'pharmacist' to all registered persons. It was also responsible for introducing the restriction on corporate bodies relating to use of the term 'chemist and druggist' only when the superintendent was a qualified pharmacist who was a member of the board of directors.

Membership of the Pharmaceutical Society remained voluntary until the Pharmacy Act 1933 introduced compulsory registration as either a 'pharmaceutical chemist' or a 'chemist and druggist' in order to practise. Later legislation, the Pharmacy Act 1954, established the single register of pharmaceutical chemists. A separate register of pharmacy premises had originally been introduced in a voluntary manner in 1936 and remains a current requirement of the Medicines Act. Regulation of company ownership of pharmacies is also covered by the Medicines Act 1968.

The 1933 Act also introduced a requirement for a mechanism to deal with removal from the register in cases of unprofessional behaviour by members. An inspectorate was set up to visit pharmacies and to investigate allegations of misbehaviour. A statutory disciplinary committee appointed to consider misconduct and criminal convictions of members considered such cases. The first case relating to an issue of being in control of a pharmacy whilst under the influence of alcohol was dealt with in 1936.

Restricted title

Titles such as 'pharmaceutical chemist' and 'pharmaceutist' were restricted by the Pharmacy Act of 1852 to persons who had passed the Society's major exam (with the title 'chemist and druggist' reserved for those who had taken the minor qualification). The Medicines Act 1968 makes it a criminal offence to use the title 'pharmacist' and others like 'pharmacy' unless legally entitled to do so under British law. The major examination followed 3 years of study and was intended for pharmacy owners, whereas the minor, more practical exam took place after 2 years' part-time study.

It is important that student pharmacists and non-pharmacist directors of bodies corporate owning pharmacies take care not to give an impression that they are registered pharmacists. To do so would be committing a crime and could result in prosecution. Only persons whose names are included on the register of pharmaceutical chemists compiled annually by the RPSGB until 2010 were entitled to use the restricted title 'pharmacist'. From 2010 the duty to compile a register of pharmacists was taken over by the General Pharmaceutical Council (GPhC: see below for details). The split of the RPSGB into a professional leadership body and a separate regulatory body has recently caused consternation amongst some pharmacists, particularly those reaching retirement age. Registration with the GPhC is restricted to practising pharmacists whereas previously membership of the RPSGB was available to practising and non-practising pharmacists. This means that, in future, once pharmacists have retired and ceased to practise they are no longer entitled to use the restricted title or register with the regulatory body.

General Pharmaceutical Council

The RPSGB ceased to exist in relation to regulation of the profession in 2010. This was as a result of government policy – *Trust, Assurance and Safety* – regarding healthcare professional regulation, prompted by the failure of professional regulation following a series of incidents concerning various healthcare professionals. These included the activities and subsequent inquiries into Dr Harold Shipman, the Manchester general practitioner who was responsible for the murder of many of his elderly patients over a prolonged period of time (Smith 2004). Another was the findings of the Kennedy report into the actions of paediatric surgeons at Bristol Royal Infirmary, whose operations on young children had a high mortality rate (Kennedy 2001).

Legislation under section 60 of the Health Act 1999 was drafted. This Pharmacy Order 2009 set out the arrangements for the ongoing regulation of pharmacy and the establishment of the GPhC (see below).

Under the new arrangements, the GPhC takes on the registration requirements for the profession; this includes the registration of pharmacists, pharmacy technicians and pharmacy premises. The pharmacy inspectorate transferred to this new organisation which is responsible to the Department of Health. The order is also responsible for introducing a requirement for compulsory recording and monitoring continuing professional development. It is expected that a further requirement will be introduced within the next few years, that of revalidation in order to remain on the practising register. The Pharmacy Order gives the GPhC the power to enforce the fitness to practise arrangements: this includes the arrangements for conducting investigations and fitness to practise committees, as well as registration appeals committees, which take place in accordance with rules set out under the auspices of the regulations/order.

The Privy Council determines the constitution of the council. The council's duties include maintaining the register of pharmacists, pharmacy technicians and pharmacy premises. For this purpose a secretary and registrar are appointed. Other roles include determining standards for premises and registrants to protect the safety of patients and the public, to establish standards and requirements for education and training and to ensure maintenance of fitness to practise. This includes setting a code of ethics and other practice guidance or standards.

Statutory instrument 2007 no. 289, the Pharmacists and Pharmacy Technicians Order 2007, governs conditions for registration. Qualifications to apply for registration include the need to obtain a degree in pharmacy from an accredited school of pharmacy followed by a 52-week preregistration period and passing the registration examination. These procedures for registration are set out in the order and include the requirement for a signed declaration of fitness to practise, payment of a designated retention fee and an undertaking to maintain up-to-date professional knowledge and keep records of continuing professional development activities undertaken. The governing legislation for the GPhC is the Pharmacy Order 2009. It is not expected that the registration requirements will be vastly changed, although additional requirements may be added, such as the need to be a currently practising pharmacist. In order to continue to practise as a pharmacist registration with the GPhC is compulsory.

The course curriculum for accredited pharmacy degrees must meet the requirements of the relevant European directives (85/432/EEC and 85/433/EEC). One of the effects of this is that pharmacists registered in countries that are part of the European Economic Area are eligible to register and practise in Great Britain under article 44 of European directive 2005/36/EC.

Previously, reciprocal arrangements had existed that had allowed pharmacists registered in Australia, New Zealand and South Africa to complete a short period of preregistration before being eligible to apply for registration. The system worked in reverse for British pharmacists wishing to apply to register in these countries. The last of these arrangements ceased in 2006.

Pharmacists qualified in countries other than the European Economic Area may still apply for registration in Britain. They must apply under specific arrangements set up by the professional regulator. This includes completion of the Overseas Pharmacist Assessment Programme, application for which will require details of the overseas qualification and registration; this will be followed by a period of preregistration training prior to taking the preregistration examination.

For those pharmacists who have undertaken additional qualifications to become authorised prescribers the register is annotated to indicate whether they are a supplementary prescriber or an independent prescriber. In addition the register entry can indicate whether any warnings or conditions are attached to that registration as a result of fitness to practise determinations.

The draft Pharmacy Order of 2009 began its consultation phase in December 2008. This was in accordance with the requirements of section 60 of the Health Act 1999, which allows legislative amendments to statutes and devolved legislation to permit changes to be made that relate to the regulation of healthcare professionals. This is done by means of an Order in Council. This particular draft order built on the recommendations of the White Paper *Trust, Assurance and Safety – The Regulation of Health Professionals in the 21st Century,* which called for the establishment of the GPhC. Its intention is to modernise and strengthen the regulation of healthcare professionals, including pharmacists and pharmacy technicians, in order to ensure confidence in the regulatory bodies and to protect patients and the public.

The Pharmacy Order sets out the main objectives for the new regulatory organisation as well as the framework for governance and constitutional arrangements and how the transition from the RPSGB was to be handled. The main objective of the GPhC is to protect, promote and maintain the health, safety and well-being of members of the public, particularly those who use pharmacy services, by ensuring that these services adhere to standards that are considered necessary for safe and effective practice.

The GPhC as a professional regulator is required by the government to be seen to be independent and impartial in its actions. The Council of a regulatory body is required to focus on strategy and oversight and is similar in size and role to those of other healthcare professional regulatory organisations. It is required to have at least equal numbers of lay and professional members and these are to be independently appointed rather than elected. The arrangements for membership, term of office and other provisions relating to membership or appointment to the Council are set out in a constitution order, a statutory instrument. The Council is required to have at least one member who lives or works in each of the countries that it covers.

The registers previously maintained by the RPSGB have been taken over by the GPhC. These have been combined to form a single register of pharmacists, pharmacy technicians and pharmacy premises, although these will be set out as separate parts as determined by the Council. The requirements for the register will be subject to amendment to allow for future practice developments to be taken into account and regulated. This is similar to the addition of the provision to annotate the previous register of pharmacists to indicate that a registrant was an authorised prescriber.

The GPhC has a function in setting and enforcing standards for safe practice in registered retail pharmacies. This covers both the standards of the premises or environment as well as the individuals working there. It is anticipated that enforcement powers such as improvement notices, fines, disqualification and removal of

KeyPoints

The main functions of the GPhC include:
- the registration of competent, qualified practitioners, including arrangements for temporary registration in emergencies
- setting and securing standards of practice, education and training, continuing professional development and conduct
- setting up and maintaining fitness to practise procedures
- registration, regulation and inspection of pharmacy premises.

(Reproduced from Department of Health, 2008.)

registration will be in place to assist in these aspects of the Council's role in addition to the continued role and function of the pharmacy inspectorate. A fitness to practise mechanism exists to deal with individual registrants and representatives of bodies corporate. The procedures in place continue to be those recently established by the RPSGB, although there is provision in the Order for these to be amended if necessary (see below for details of the fitness to practise procedures).

Professional representative body

Following the removal of the regulatory aspects of its role from the charter, the RPSGB remains with a continued function in its capacity of professional leadership and support for its membership. This has required a number of changes in its constitution, many of which continue to be settled. Although a major change is that membership of the professional body is not mandatory, this means that an individual does not need to be a member to be able to practise as a pharmacist. The new professional leadership body has stated that it is committed to representing and leading its members. In addition, it speaks for its membership, aims to raise the status and profile of the profession of pharmacy and represents the interests of its members to the GPhC, government and patients. It continues to provide and is further developing its role in relation to professional development and training. This includes support for pharmacists in relation to the continuing professional development and future revalidation requirements of the professional regulator as a condition of registration. In addition the professional body continues to provide library and information and advisory services for its membership as well as guidance on good practice. Further functions are the continued publication of professional journals relevant to the practice of pharmacy and the provision of a pharmacist support service for those in difficult times.

A national assembly, drawn from representatives of each of the three national pharmacy boards by nomination, that is England, Wales and Scotland, oversees the professional body. Each national pharmacy board is made up of a number of elected members, most of whom are pharmacists, although the constitution of each board can vary. The English board has places reserved for specified sectoral representation, and all have lay representation. In addition to the nominated members from the national boards the assembly includes a pharmaceutical scientist, an academic and a lay member. The assembly members elect the president.

Professional accountability and responsibility

In addition to abiding by legislation, registration as a professional practitioner carries with it the requirement to accept professional accountability and responsibility for practice. As a practising professional, the individual pharmacist has a legal duty of care towards his or her clients or patients. A pharmacist's training and experience mean that he or she is an expert on medicines and their use. When called upon to provide a service or advice to patients the pharmacist has a duty in law to ensure that his or her knowledge is used to ensure that so far as is possible no harm will come to the user or recipient. For example, if patients are purchasing medicines from a pharmacy they can expect safe information and advice relating to their choice, whereas a customer purchasing the same medicine from a supermarket with no pharmacy department cannot rely on a duty of care in relation to any advice provided on that medicine's use by the supermarket sales staff.

Professional responsibility and accountability are not just covered by legal requirements. Many of the standards required of individual pharmacists, whatever their actual role, are set out in the form of a code of conduct or ethics and guidance on professional practice. These are considered in detail in Chapter 9. However it is important to include mention of this here as the fitness to practise mechanisms of the regulatory body include an expectation of adherence to the code or guidance in their remit when determining unacceptable behaviour or actions by registrants.

Fitness to practise – see Health Act 2006

The current fitness to practise mechanisms were introduced by the 2007 statutory instrument number 289, also known as the Pharmacist and Pharmacy Technician Order 2007. The Pharmacy Order 2009 included provision for these procedures to continue throughout the devolution of the regulatory functions of the RPSGB to the GPhC in 2010 (see above for details of this change).

One of the key issues relating to the fitness to practise procedure is concerned with establishing whether the fitness to practise of an individual is impaired. Others require that procedures are followed in the interest of the public and that hearings are fairly conducted under common law and the requirements of the European Convention of Human Rights.

The purposes of the sanctions available under the fitness to practise procedures are to protect the public, to maintain public confidence in the profession and to maintain standards. In imposing sanctions the committees must act in a

KeyPoints

According to the Pharmacy and Pharmacy Technician's Order 2007, a person's fitness to practise may be impaired by reason of any of following:
- misconduct
- deficient professional performance
- adverse physical or mental health
- failure to comply with reasonable requirement by assessor
- a conviction for a criminal offence – British Isles
- a police caution – British Isles
- finding impaired fitness to practise by health or social care regulatory body.

way that is fair and reasonable, consider the full range of sanctions available to them and take into account the wider public interest as well as those of the individual practitioner. This is called proportionality and ensures that the sanction imposed is appropriate to its purpose or objectives.

The procedures are operated through three committees: (1) the Investigating Committee; (2) the Disciplinary Committee; and (3) the Health Committee. Full details of the operation of the process were first set out in the statutory instrument 2007 number 442, The Royal Pharmaceutical Society of Great Britain (Fitness to Practise and Disqualification etc. Rules) Order of Council 2007. A brief outline of the processes and available sanctions is set out here.

Complaints received by the regulatory body are considered in relation to fitness to practise issues and if it appears that this is impaired, the case will be put to the Investigating Committee. This committee will review the documentary evidence and, if it believes that there is a real prospect of a finding of impairment, it will refer the case for consideration by either the Disciplinary or the Health Committee. It can ask for further investigations to take place or for medical reports to be obtained. This committee is supported by legal and clinical advisers who have no voting rights and any decision is made on the basis of a simple majority. Other than accepting undertakings from pharmacists, issuing a warning and giving advice, the main outcome from this committee is to refer a case to either the Health or the Disciplinary Committee. They will do this having taken into account issues such as the harm caused or potential for harm, personal health and behaviour, any attempts made to cover up or obstruct investigation of the issue, and any previous history.

The Health Committee receives evidence in writing and in person to determine whether fitness to practise is impaired and what, if any, penalty should be imposed. It operates to the civil standard of proof (see Chapter 1), which means that the decision must be made on the balance of probabilities and a simple majority is required. The committee sits in private and is assisted by non-voting legal and clinical advisers. It is up to the regulator to present the evidence to prove its case. Even when the Health Committee reaches a decision that fitness to practise is not impaired, it can still issue a warning or give advice to anybody appropriate (for example, a superintendent pharmacist about employing the individual). Where the fitness to practise is found to be impaired the sanctions include issuing a warning that can be included into the register, imposition of conditions for a period of up to 3 years or suspension from the register for up to 12 months. Conditions imposed or suspension can in certain circumstances take immediate effect; otherwise there is a 28-day period in which the individual can lodge an appeal to the High Court about the decision.

The Disciplinary Committee's role is to determine either that fitness to practise is impaired or that a corporate body has committed misconduct and whether any sanctions should be imposed. The regulator has the task of proving its case and the standard of proof is the same as for the Health Committee, that is, on the balance of probabilities. The Disciplinary Committee takes evidence orally as well as in written form and usually sits in public. If it believes that the case relates to health issues then it can refer to the Health Committee. Only when the case has been proved and aggravating and mitigating issues have been considered will a sanction be imposed. These include: issuing a warning and including this in the register; issuing advice to appropriate persons; imposing conditions for a period of up to 3 years; suspension from the register for up to 12 months; or removal from the register. As for the Health Committee, conditions imposed or suspension can in certain circumstances take immediate effect; otherwise there is a 28-day period in which the individual can lodge an appeal to the High Court about the decision.

Once removed from the register an individual cannot apply for return to the register until a period of 5 years has elapsed and, if unsuccessful at the first attempt, a further period of 12 months must pass before a reapplication will be considered. The application will be heard by the Disciplinary Committee which will only allow it if the applicant is able to prove that he or she is entitled to register and is fit to practise. In addition conditions on practice may be imposed for up to 3 years.

One further committee exists with responsibility in relation to registration. This is the Registration Appeals Committee, which considers applications for registration that have been turned down by the secretary and registrar due to impaired fitness to practise, such as issues relating to health or character. For example, this can be a preregistration student who has disclosed a criminal conviction or health issue in his or her application which will require further investigation by the committee to determine whether to quash the decision or give a different direction. Any applicant for registration is legally obliged to provide information relating to

KeyPoints

The profession was established over 150 years ago with the purpose of representing the interests of practising pharmacists and protection of the public. Its roles evolved over time into a joint professional and regulatory organisation.

Many of the titles associated with the profession, such as pharmacist and chemist, are restricted. This means that it is illegal for the titles to be used if not legally entitled to do so.

The General Pharmaceutical Council (GPhC) replaces the regulatory functions of the Royal Pharmaceutical Society of Great Britain (RPSGB) from 2010. This change was brought about in line with government policy in relation to safety and standards of all healthcare professions.

Pharmacists' interests continue to be supported by the RPSGB as a professional representative body. It provides a voice for pharmacy, publications and opportunities for continuing professional development, amongst other services and functions.

As a professional practitioner, pharmacists and pharmacy technicians are both accountable and responsible for their working practices.

Fitness to practise procedures are the responsibility of the professional regulatory body. They operate through a number of formal committees that have various sanctions available to them. The Commission for Healthcare Regulatory Excellence (CHRE) oversees this process.

fitness to practise and, as a potential healthcare professional, is not subject to the Rehabilitation of Offenders Act 1974. This means that those criminal convictions that are more than 10 years old, which in other aspects of life might be considered to be spent, will still be considered.

The whole process is overseen by the Commission for Healthcare Regulatory Excellence (CHRE), to whom all decisions by healthcare regulatory bodies must be reported within 28 days of any hearing. The CHRE is an independent body accountable to Parliament. Its role is to review performance or monitor health profession regulators: it has the power to refer decisions that it considers to be too lenient and failing to protect the public interests to the High Court or Court of Sessions in Scotland.

In time the role in hearing fitness to practise cases will be transferred and taken over by the new Office of Health Professions adjudicator, as established by the Health and Social Care Act 2008. The GPhC will then continue to investigate alleged cases of impaired fitness to practise and will retain its prosecution functions.

Self-assessment

1. **When was the Pharmaceutical Society established and by whom?**
a. 1841 by Jacob Bell
b. 1843 by William Allen
c. 1933 by Theophilus Redwood
d. 1954 by Joseph Ince

2. **Which one of the following was not an aim of the newly established Pharmaceutical Society?**
a. To benefit the public
b. To introduce a scheme of pharmacy education
c. To protect the interests of pharmacists
d. To establish a register of practising pharmacists

3. **When did it become a legal requirement for all practising pharmacists to register with the Pharmaceutical Society?**
a. 1853
b. 1868
c. 1933
d. 1954

4. **Identify the relevant legislation that required this registration.**
a. The Pharmacy Act 1852
b. The Pharmacy Act 1868
c. The Pharmacy Act 1933
d. The Pharmacy Act 1954

5. What year was the title 'Royal' granted to the Pharmaceutical
    Society?
a. 1841
b. 1843
c. 1954
d. 1988

6. Which of the following is not one of the roles and functions of the
    General Pharmaceutical Council (GPhC)?
a. Registration of competent, qualified practitioners
b. Setting and securing standards of practice, education and training,
    continuing professional development and conduct
c. Setting up and maintaining fitness to practise procedures
d. Maintenance of a benevolent fund for pharmacists and their
    dependants

7. Name the legislation which governs the operation of the GPhC that
    came into force in 2009.
a. The Pharmacy and Pharmacy Technicians Order 2007
b. The Pharmacy Order 2007
c. The Pharmacy and Pharmacy Technicians Order 2009
d. The Pharmacy Order 2009

8. Which one of the following is not a relevant committee under the
    fitness to practise mechanisms?
a. Health Committee
b. Investigating Committee
c. Law and Ethics Committee
d. Disciplinary Committee

9. What is the period of time that must elapse before a person removed
    from the register is allowed to apply for restoration?
a. No time limit applies
b. 2 years from the date of removal
c. 5 years from the date of removal
d. 7 years from the date of removal

10. Which of the following is not considered to be impairment in relation
    to fitness to practise?
a. Misconduct
b. A police caution received in any European country
c. Deficient professional performance
d. Adverse physical or mental health

References

Department of Health. White Paper. *Trust, Assurance and Safety – The Regulation of
Health Professionals in the 21st Century.* London: Department of Health, 2007.

Department of Health. Creating a new professional regulator for pharmacy (2008). Available online at: www.dh.gov.uk.

Kennedy I. *The Bristol Royal Infirmary Inquiry: Learning from Bristol*. Cm 5207(1). London: The Stationery Office, 2001.

Smith J. *The Shipman Inquiry: The Fourth Report: The Regulation of Controlled Drugs in the Community*. Command Paper Cm 6249. London: The Stationery Office, 2004.

Further reading

Anderson S (ed.) *Making Medicines*. London: Pharmaceutical Press, 2005.

Appelbe GE, Wingfield J. *Dale and Appelbe's Pharmacy Law and Ethics*, 8th edn. London: Pharmaceutical Press, 2005.

Holloway SWF. *Royal Pharmaceutical Society of Great Britain 1841–1991*. London: Pharmaceutical Press, 1991.

chapter 9
Ethics and professionalism

Overview

Upon completion of this chapter, you should be able to:
- describe the Code of Ethics, including an awareness of its background; why it is needed; description of the current Code of Ethics, who it relates to, its purpose and standing in law
- demonstrate awareness of the principles of healthcare ethics, including the four basic principles in medical ethics: beneficence, non-maleficence, autonomy and justice
- discuss the meaning of confidentiality in relation to ethics of pharmacy practice
- be aware of the ethical issues regarding patient consent
- understand the meaning of concordance and the rights of patients in relation to their treatment
- consider the issues raised by conflicts between personal and professional views.

Code of Ethics

The Code of Ethics is not law, although its enforcement is via the fitness to practise committees. The Pharmacy and Pharmacy Technician Order 2007 introduced the first legal requirement for the publication of guidance to standards of conduct, practice and performance. This includes the Code of Ethics and standards for guidance, published each year in the *Medicines Ethics and Practice* guide (Snell 2009).

The requirements of the Code of Ethics lie somewhere over and above the strict letter of the law. But what is ethics? It has been defined as the science of morals and there are various levels of morality to which we are each bound: personal; society; ethnic community; and professional. It relates to how we behave towards each other and sets rules by which people exist in harmony. It also concerns the values that lie behind making moral choices and that is very much one of the key uses towards which the Code of Ethics is put, as an aid to assisting in the resolution of professional challenges.

According to Bennion, writing in 1969 in *Professional Ethics*, a professional code is the judgement of the profession on how its members should conduct themselves.

A code of ethics is an expression of the conduct that is considered to be 'right' and the values that underpin this. As views of acceptable norms in general society change, so a profession's views will change with time. For example, the advertising of condoms and contraceptives that is nowadays considered to be perfectly acceptable was very restricted in the mid 20th century. The 1964 Code of Ethics stated that 'there should be no exhibition of contraceptives in a pharmacy or any reference direct or indirect by way of advertisement, notice, showcard or otherwise that they are sold there other than a notice approved by the Council bearing the words 'Family Planning Requisites'.

The Pharmaceutical Society of Great Britain was founded in 1841 and although there were calls for a code of ethics as early as the 1850s, prompted by the adoption of a code in the USA, the Society did not attempt to formulate one for many years.

It was not until 1939 that the first code of conduct was adopted by the Society. The 1933 Pharmacy and Poisons Act had resulted in the setting-up of the Statutory Committee to deal with disciplinary or misconduct matters and guidance was needed to members as to what constituted misconduct. This first code was entitled the Statement on Matters of Professional Conduct and it included restrictions on advertising, sale of items of misuse, substitution and pricing and reflected the main existing matters of concern to the profession.

As times changed, the code had to be amended to reflect the moral concerns of the relevant time. It underwent a number of reviews at approximately 10-year intervals and at times was supplemented by additional statements and guidance. The 1984 revision was retitled to become the Code of Ethics. The current Code of Ethics was adopted in May 2007 and for the first time covered pharmacy technicians as well as pharmacists.

This latest version of the code consists of seven compulsory principles that must be followed by all practising pharmacists and pharmacy technicians. These principles are supplemented by supporting explanations to expand on and illustrate those aspects of practice that are covered by a particular ethical principle.

KeyPoints

The seven principles of the Code of Ethics
1. Make the care of patients your first concern.
2. Exercise professional judgement in the interests of patients and the public.
3. Show respect for others.
4. Encourage patients to participate in decisions about their care.
5. Develop your professional knowledge and competence.
6. Be honest and trustworthy.
7. Take responsibility for your working practices.

These principles and their explanations also provide guidance as to the standard of practice or conduct that is required and all practitioners are responsible for applying the Code of Ethics to their roles. They can be used to inform service users and other healthcare professionals of the standards expected of the pharmacy profession.

The code and its supplementary statements will not cover all eventualities and indeed these will not all be applicable to every situation that can arise in pharmacy. On occasion dilemmas or challenges occur in practice when one or more principles or an ethical principle and a legal requirement may contradict each other. When this situation occurs the individual practitioner will have to work out how to apply the available information to the situation in order to determine what action to take. The use of professional judgement will come into play (see Chapter 10 for examples) and the individual must be prepared to accept professional responsibility and accountability and should be able to justify his or her eventual action.

Principle 6.6 of the Code of Ethics requires compliance with legal requirements, mandatory professional standards and accepted best practice guidance. This is provided in the form of an additional series of standards documents, the *Professional Standards and Guidance* documents (Royal Pharmaceutical Society of Great Britain 2007). Nine standards documents are available, although this number may change in response to the need for guidance in relation to new services or issues affecting practice.

The purpose of these documents is to expand and illustrate the application of the seven principles of the Code of Ethics to the practice situation. It is therefore important that all pharmacists and pharmacy technicians are familiar with the requirements of the *Professional Standards and Guidance* documents in addition to the Code of Ethics. They must also ensure that they remain up to date with any changes and amendments to these and apply them to their practice.

KeyPoints

Professional Standards and Guidance documents cover the following aspects of practice:
- For those in positions of authority
- Patient consent
- Patient confidentiality
- Sale and supply of medicines
- Advertising medicines and professional services
- Internet pharmacy services
- Pharmacist prescribers
- Continuing professional development
- Responsible pharmacist.

Tip

Professional standards that are compulsory use the word 'must' whilst those that are good practice are indicated by the use of 'should'.

This does not mean that guidance can be ignored: an individual might be called upon to justify why he or she chose to ignore best practice guidance!

For many years a breach of the requirements of the Code of Ethics has formed the basis of a complaint of professional misconduct or impairment in fitness to practise. In any disciplinary case the specific circumstances concerning the offence are taken into account and the disciplinary procedures or committees are not limited just to the matters included in the code. Enforcement of the Code of Ethics and associated guidance lies in the first place with the pharmacy inspectorate who, in the course of their work routinely visiting registered pharmacy premises, will identify some complaints. Other sources of complaint include members of the public, primary care organisations, the police and trading standards officers (see Chapter 8).

Student Code of Ethics

Since autumn 2009 university students enrolled on an accredited pharmacy course have been subject to a student version of the Code of Ethics and in 2010 it became a requirement that they were also subject to fitness to practise mechanisms operated by the educational institute. The outcome of any fitness to practise investigations, when they indicate possible impairment, is notified to the professional regulator and considered if and when the individual seeks to gain entry to the register.

KeyPoints

Beauchamp and Childress's principles of biomedical ethics (the Georgetown mantra)
- Beneficence
- Non-maleficence
- Respect for autonomy
- Justice.

Principles of healthcare ethics

Many of the principles of the Code of Ethics are founded in the work of Beauchamp and Childress (2008) from Georgetown, USA. Their work established four basic biomedical ethical principles that together work to bring order and understanding to more specific principles of healthcare ethics. Whilst knowing these and what they encompass may not actually provide an answer to ethical problems in practice, they do provide a basis for trying to work out the answer. What is more, this basis is widely recognised by other healthcare practitioners.

Whilst the terminology can seem difficult or even incomprehensible, these four principles are really very straightforward. Beneficence is all about doing good, particularly doing what will benefit others, such as the patient and anyone else affected by an ethical decision. This is seen in the first principle of the Code of Ethics, where care of the patient is the first concern, and also in the second, that calls for the pharmacist or technician to act in the interests of the patient.

Non-maleficence is the duty to do no harm. This is not the same as taking no action since this in itself could result in harm being caused. This principle works to moderate that of beneficence since if doing good for one person caused harm to others, overall the action cannot be said to be good. In ethical decision making it is important to establish who may be affected by any decision. In pharmacy a simple example of this principle would be the refusal of a pharmacist to sell a medicine if the pharmacist thought it was being purchased for a wrong reason.

Respect for autonomy is about allowing individuals to have the right to make decisions for themselves. Again, this right is tempered if one person's decision was likely to have harmful effects on others. It also depends on the individual's ability to appreciate and understand the issues at stake.

The final one of these four principles is justice. This is about fairness and providing for the same level of service or care regardless of who the recipient is. It is about not judging the reasons behind a patient's need such as might occur in relation to providing services to drug misusers.

The next section of this chapter aims to cover some of the key aspects of the Code of Ethics that often cause specific challenges in pharmacy practice. The full details of each are set out in the *Professional Standards and Guidance* documents, but a brief outline is included here for the following: consent, confidentiality, concordance, the rights of patients (personal versus professional views) and sale of medicines liable to misuse.

Consent

Principle 3 of the Code of Ethics requires that respect is shown for others. This includes the legal and professional duty to obtain consent from patients for any services or treatments you provide for them or to use any information that you obtain from them. For any consent to be valid the individual who is consenting must be deemed to be capable of making the decision; must be acting voluntarily; must have been provided with sufficient information; and must be capable of weighing up that information. This process is called informed consent. A competent patient has a right to refuse any services or treatment offered or to refuse permission for you to use information for any other purpose. The basic biomedical ethics principle involved is that of respect of the patient's autonomy.

For a pharmacist one of the key issues will be the quantity and quality of any information provided and how this is communicated to the patient. Consent need not be obtained in writing, although if an invasive procedure is being performed this might be wise. Obviously the matter of ability to consent will depend on the patient: young children and mentally impaired patients may not be able to give consent. The assessment of capacity to consent can be challenging and if unsure specialist advice must be sought. Generally all adults are assumed to have capacity to provide consent, as are children aged over 16. For younger children the assessment can be more difficult; this is often seen in relation to the supply of emergency hormonal contraception under a patient group direction to girls as young as 12. However guidance from the courts is available in the decision of the case of Gillick v. West Norfolk and Wisbech Area Health Authority in 1985. This stated that a person under the age of 16 can give consent if he or she has sufficient understanding and intelligence to enable him or her to understand fully what is proposed.

Confidentiality

Principle 3 of the Code of Ethics also contains a requirement to use patient information only for the purpose for which it was obtained. This is in addition to the legal requirements of data protection (see Chapter 7). Healthcare professionals, including pharmacists, are often trusted by patients to keep confidences and it is this trust that enables patients to share private information to assist in the provision of appropriate care and services. The basis of confidentiality is the ethical principle of autonomy, that is, the rights of the individual patient. However this can at times be confused when the patient is unable to give consent to share confidential information with other interested parties. Of course those interested parties should only receive information if they need to know it for the benefit of the patient; this becomes more difficult when there is a greater public health issue to protect other members of the public.

The Children Act 2004 and previous legislation place a requirement on organisations to ensure that in carrying out their functions they safeguard and protect the welfare of children. Pharmacy staff may, during the course of their work, be alerted to the possibility of a child suffering neglect or abuse. If worried about the possibility of significant harm or potential abuse these concerns must be notified to the Social Services. If it is thought that the child's parent or guardian may be involved with the abuse the matter should not be discussed with them as this could put the child at greater risk. Specific guidance for pharmacists on this matter is provided by the Royal Pharmaceutical Society of Great Britain. This deals with the issue of breaching patient confidence and when to report sexual activity in the underage child.

Concordance

The principles of concordance also involve consideration of the autonomy of the patient as well as that of beneficence. The older paternalistic approach to medicine involved the practitioner utilising his or her knowledge to decide what was the best treatment for the patient. The patient's views were rarely taken into account, sometimes leading to issues about compliance. The introduction of principles based on patient autonomy has resulted in patients being involved in the choices of treatment or care available and the development of mutual trust. Concordance means coming to an agreement, in this case an agreement between the patient and practitioner. If the patient's views are respected the health professional has a duty to ensure that he or she provides the patient with sufficient information to make that agreement. This is similar to the requirements for consent, although not perhaps quite so formal. It is important to recognise that the patient has the ultimate right not to agree to a certain form of treatment. It is good practice to make a record of any such discussions and decisions just in case there was a possibility of an allegation of negligence against a professional practitioner. This is more likely to be the case for a prescribing or special interest pharmacist.

Personal versus professional views

Everyone has their own moral make-up based perhaps on the values acquired during their upbringing. Often this is affected by their culture and/or religion. Occasionally these personal moral values can conflict with those of the profession. In such cases the individual practitioner is bound by the requirements of the professional Code of Ethics to put the interests of his or her patient first. Sometimes this can be achieved without too much difficulty, such as signposting a patient to a nearby pharmacy that can provide the service being sought. However if there is no nearby pharmacy the situation is not so easy. A difficult decision will have to be made and justified within the accepted behaviour for that profession. The pharmacist has a duty of care to the patient and other customers: if this duty is breached and harm is caused as a result, a professional might be subjected to the civil claim of negligence. In this case the guidance for acceptable actions would be the Bolam test. This principle was established in relation to a medical case taken against Friern Hospital Management Trust in 1957. This indicates that the action is not considered to be negligent if the standard of care provided is that of the ordinary skilled man exercising and professing to have that skill. This means that where a pharmacist is following commonly accepted good practice within the profession, any harm caused by his or her actions should not be considered to be negligent. This makes the idea of following current published practice guidance a good one since doing so should provide a legal defence.

Preventing misuse of medicines

Pharmacists are more usually concerned with the 'proper use' of a medicine and can often be surprised to learn of abuse associated with a product. In addition the person using a medicine for the wrong purpose may not be aware of the harm that can be caused by a readily available medicine. This is often the case, for example, when painkillers are used to treat a headache on a regular basis. It is quite likely that what ends up being 'treated' is an analgesic withdrawal headache, thus creating a vicious circle that is difficult for the customer both to understand and to break.

The reasons for misusing medicines are many and varied. They range from ignorance about the effect of the medicine and its proper use through the masking of symptoms of a more serious illness, to physical and psychological dependence. Other reasons can include peer

KeyPoints

The Code of Ethics and its associated documents have the prime purpose of providing guidance as to the expected standards of behaviour. It also has a role in informing others, such as the public and patients, other healthcare professionals and the disciplinary process.

The advantages of a Code of Ethics are that it is unique and relevant to the profession, it can be kept up to date without a need for legislative changes and it can assist with the analysis of situations and help with the resolution of dilemmas.

Finally, it meets the obligations under The Pharmacists and Pharmacist Technicians Order 2007, the Pharmacy Order 2009 and other relevant legislation to set out the standards of practice, conduct and performance.

The Code of Ethics is supplemented by additional professional standards documents and guidance relating to specific aspects of practice.

Four basic ethical principles relating to healthcare are set out by Beauchamp and Childress: beneficence, non-maleficence, respect for autonomy and justice.

pressure, enhancing athletic performance, to alter mood – producing either euphoria or relaxation – and as an adjunct to enhance the effect of other drugs or alcohol.

To comply with the professional guidance requirements pharmacists have a duty to make sure that they know which products are misused, to ensure that standard operating procedures deal with issues arising from requests for such products and to train counter staff. It is well accepted that pharmacists must prevent the misuse of medicines, although in practice this often results in a dilemma – 'whether to sell a medicine or not' – and it is often difficult to differentiate the misuser from the legitimate user.

Self-assessment

1. In what year did the Pharmaceutical Society first adopt a Code of Ethics?
a. 1841
b. 1933
c. 1939
d. 1941

2. Which of the following is not a principle in the Code of Ethics?
a. Show respect for others
b. Professional services may not be advertised
c. Be honest and trustworthy
d. Take responsibility for working practices

3. Which one of the following is not one of Beauchamp and Childress's four basic principles of biomedical ethics?
a. Beneficence
b. Non-maleficence
c. Respect for autonomy
d. Patient consent

4. What does the word 'non-maleficence' mean?
a. Do not hate
b. Do no harm
c. Do no good
d. Treat individuals equally

5. Which of the following is not required for informed consent?
a. The individual is at least 21 years old
b. The individual is deemed to be capable
c. The individual is acting voluntarily
d. The individual has been provided with sufficient information

6. **Which of the following would not be a suitable method of disposal for confidential waste?**
a. Shredding computer CD backup discs
b. Incinerating all dispensary paper waste
c. Obliterating patient information on paper waste using a marker pen
d. Removing dispensing labels from returned medicines and disposing of these in the waste bin

7. **Concordance is the process of:**
a. Shared decision making between the prescriber and the patient
b. The patient following the prescriber's treatment instructions
c. A patient failing to comply with treatment instructions
d. Matching patients' behaviour to prescriber recommendations

8. **Which of the following is not a necessary element in relation to proving a claim of negligence?**
a. Breach of an established duty of care
b. Injury or harm that has caused loss or damage
c. Injury caused by failure to follow advice provided
d. Damage was a result of malpractice

9. **Which of the following is not a possible reason for intentional misuse of a medicine?**
a. Purchase of a medicine to treat a licensed indication
b. Request to use a medicine outside its licensed indication
c. A patient continuing to use an over-the-counter medicine once symptoms have resolved
d. Increasing the dose of a medicine to obtain a faster or stronger effect

10. **Which of the following is not a requirement for pharmacies in relation to the sale of medicines that can be misused?**
a. Pharmacists must make sure they know what products are likely to be misused
b. Pharmacies must have standard operating procedures covering such sales
c. The pharmacist must be directly involved with all sales of medicines that might be misused
d. Counter staff must be trained to deal with requests for medicines that might be misused

References

Beauchamp TL, Childress JF, *Principles of Biomedical Ethics*, 6th edn. New York: Oxford University Press, 2008.
Bennion FAR. *Professional Ethics.* London: Charles Knight, 1969.

Royal Pharmaceutical Society of Great Britain. *Professional Standards and Guidance*. London: Royal Pharmaceutical Society of Great Britain, 2007.
Snell M (ed.) *Medicines Ethics and Practice: A Guide for Pharmacists and Pharmacy Technicians*, 33rd edn. London: Pharmaceutical Press, 2009.

Further reading

Hope T, Savulescu J, Hendrick J. *Medical Ethics and Law: The Core Curriculum*. London: Churchill Livingstone, 2003.
Howard P, Bogle J. *Medical Law and Ethics*. Oxford: Blackwell, 2005.
Wingfield J, Badcott D. *Pharmacy Ethics and Decision Making*. London: Pharmaceutical Press, 2007.

chapter 10

Pharmacy practice problems, challenges and dilemmas

Overview

Upon completion of this chapter, you should be able to:
- identify the relevant facts in a practice problem or dilemma
- identify the key issues and prioritise these in the light of any legislation or guidance
- develop options for action.

This chapter provides an outline of a procedure for dealing with difficult practice decisions. It includes case studies to work through and discuss with friends and colleagues. Sample answers are provided along with the answers to self-assessment questions from other chapters of the book. However the answers provided are potential outcomes only and other options may be available. As most of the scenarios contain ethical decision-making problems it should be remembered that there is often no one right or wrong outcome. You may identify other issues relevant to the situation and/or prioritise the issues differently. In considering the cases provided you should consider the facts, decide what you would do as a pharmacist and be able to justify your decision.

Problems in practice can take a number of forms. Some are simple and easy to resolve, such as the lack of knowledge regarding possible interaction between two prescribed medicines. In this situation you would consult an authority such as the current edition of the *British National Formulary* or speak to a more experienced colleague. However in pharmacy practice the individual pharmacist is often working as a sole practitioner, possibly at times when other (human) resources cannot be contacted for advice, such as late at night or at weekends. In many situations the 'right' or 'correct' decision is obvious and there is little difficulty in deciding what action to take. However, difficult and challenging situations do arise and that is when it is helpful to have a decision-making process to fall back on. These challenges or dilemmas occur

KeyPoint

Definitions
- Dilemma: argument forcing opponent to choose between one of two alternatives
- Ethical dilemma: having to choose between two or more conflicting ethical principles

when the situation is complex or when it is difficult to choose between one or more options.

Resolving dilemmas is not easy but professional practice is more than just following the law or a set of rules. In pharmacy these rules are set out in the various statutes, for example the Pharmacy Act 1954, the Medicines Act 1968 and the Misuse of Drugs Act 1971, along with the professional Code of Ethics with its supplementary guidance and standards documents. Whilst the law is often clearly expressed and can be enforced in black and white terms, ethics is much more difficult to interpret.

When ethical principles are in conflict with one another or with a legal requirement it is often especially difficult to know which takes precedence. Interpretation of the principles is never easy and made more difficult by the fact that greater allowance is made for circumstances and a great many factors may have to be taken into account.

In practice pharmacists often face dilemmas such as:

- When can/should I sell codeine linctus?
- Should I sell a medicine which I know will be used for an unlicensed indication?
- Should I disclose information about a customer's medication to a third party?
- Should I ever allow untrained staff to work on the medicines counter?
- What are the maximum hours per day that I should agree to work as a pharmacist?
- Should I always recommend the cheaper, generic versions of over-the-counter preparations when these are available?
- Are there any circumstances when I could reissue an unopened, returned medicine?
- Should I recommend a particular product because I have an overstock?
- What should be the maximum number of prescriptions dispensed per pharmacist in any day?

The answer to most of these questions will be 'it depends'. The specific circumstances of each situation being faced will need to be considered and even then the answer will depend upon the individual pharmacist's experience in practice.

A decision has to be made, so how do we go about deciding what action to take? To help you make your decision you may wish to consider the following points as part of your decision-making process:

- Are there any Acts of Parliament or regulations that apply to the case?
- What is your current level of personal knowledge and competence? Will that affect your decision-making process?
- How do you apply professional ethics to the situation? How does this fit with the law?

- Who is going to be affected by any decision that you make? In what order are you going to prioritise key stakeholders in the case?
- What other options can you consider? Which option will give you the best outcome for the situation?

Identify the principles involved. To do this, gather together as many relevant facts as possible and know and be able to interpret the regulations relevant to the particular situation. This means finding out what the law or the principle/obligation actually says and what this means in relation to the situation. Has there been any published guidance or clarification that might be relevant or have there been similar cases in the past, such as disciplinary committee reports?

Once as many relevant facts as possible have been determined it is necessary to make a judgement about which take priority over others. For example, the Code of Ethics states that a pharmacist must 'make the care of patients his or her first concern' and actions which profited a pharmacy owner would therefore have a lower priority than those which provided for a greater benefit for the patient.

Consider as many outcomes as possible to work through which would provide the best outcome for all concerned. Try answering the following questions for each possible option or outcome. Who will the decision affect? How will each be affected? Is a precedent being set for the future from which it will be difficult to retreat?

Decide which outcome is best by weighing up the options you have generated and comparing the acceptability of each. If it helps and you have someone available, discuss these with other practitioners if it is appropriate to do so. Finally make the decision and take the necessary action.

Whatever the decision, be prepared to justify it and the actions taken. It is advisable to make a contemporaneous note of the event and the factors taken into account, as this can be helpful if you are later required to justify your decision.

Remember that it is your decision and no one else's. In reaching your decision you need to know your limitations and the level of risk you are prepared to take as well as the disciplinary mechanisms that exist.

The following is an example of this decision-making framework in practice. The case relates to a customer who has entered a pharmacy asking to buy some hydrocortisone cream. She says this was recommended to her by her doctor. The pharmacist notices that her eyelid is red and flaky. Should the pharmacist sell the hydrocortisone cream?

The first stage is to identify the relevant facts and principles concerned. These might include the following points:

- Hydrocortisone is licensed for pharmacy (P) sale for a limited number of indications.
- It is not licensed for use on the face.
- The licence confers responsibility and liability for harm on the manufacturer, i.e. it is a guarantee for the customer that the product should not cause harm.
- Recommendation for a use outside the licence results in the pharmacist accepting responsibility for the item sold.
- It could result in the pharmacist supplying a prescription-only medicine (POM) without a prescription.
- The fact that the doctor has recommended the purchase does not take away the pharmacist's responsibility towards the patient and the law.
- Just because the customer has a sore eye does not mean that the product is to be used on it.
- Failure to make pertinent enquiries is not an adequate defence in law and ethics.
- If forced to obtain a prescription, the customer may not be able to afford the prescription fee and then may decide to do without the cream.

It is clear that further information is required before any decision can be reached. To sell the hydrocortisone with the level of information given initially would mean that the pharmacist may be guilty at least of negligence or at worst of infringeing the law and thus be liable to prosecution.

Next prioritise the various issues. For example:

- The product supplied must be appropriate to the patient's needs and the risk of any harm being caused must be negligible.
- The pharmacist must abide by the law relating to the sale of medicines.
- Wherever possible, the product sold should be licensed for the required indication. Sometimes this is not the case, for example in relation to chemist nostrums, which are prepared in the pharmacy or with some generic preparations.
- The pharmacist should be aware of the legal status of any product supplied.
- The pharmacist should not cause undue upset to the patient.

Once priority has been assigned consider the possible outcomes for different actions that have been identified as possible:

- If the product is sold and used on the eye the pharmacist could be held negligent in the event of a claim if the patient's condition subsequently deteriorated.
- When sold for use on the eye the product has a POM status and the pharmacist could be prosecuted under the Medicines Act 1968 for supply without a prescription.

- If sold for a licensed P-category indication, the likelihood of any harm is minimal and in the event of any adverse reaction the responsibility would lie with the manufacturer.
- If the sale is refused, for whatever reason, the customer's condition may deteriorate or she may experience considerable discomfort.
- The customer may not understand the difficulties that the pharmacist is in. She may walk out and go to another pharmacy and lie in order to be able to purchase the item.
- The doctor may consider the pharmacist's attitude obstructive and this may cause a breakdown in the pharmacist–doctor relationship.

Having obtained and reviewed the possibilities it is necessary to make a decision and take some action. If further information is needed from the patient or the doctor this should be obtained. Similarly a discussion with a colleague may draw out further issues to consider or point towards a particular direction.

In this example it may have been discovered that the cream was to have been used on the face and as such you have decided that you are not prepared to supply it. You will then face another dilemma and will need to give some thought as to how you are going to explain this to a customer whose doctor has told her it is OK to use this medication and cheaper to buy than to get on prescription. You should also consider what you might say to the doctor to prevent this situation occurring on future occasions.

Finally consider the justification for your eventual decision. It is important to remember that each pharmacist is personally responsible for every professional decision that he or she takes. However the decision taken by one pharmacist is not necessarily the same decision as another pharmacist would have reached, even when given apparently similar circumstances. If the decision was particularly difficult or risky, consider making a record of the situation. This might set out your analysis of the situation, those steps that were taken to clarify it, the reasons for the decision, who was informed, and other matters. This record may be useful as a defence if disciplinary action or a claim of negligence were to result from the decision taken.

The remainder of this chapter sets out a series of 10 scenarios or case studies that require the application of much of the legal and ethical information contained in this book in order to resolve a problem or dilemma. You may also have to apply some clinical knowledge, as was the case in the example provided above. These cases have all been based on incidents that have occurred in practice or that could occur.

Read through each situation and apply the decision-making framework before checking your answers with those provided at the back of the book. But do remember that if your answers are different from those provided, this doesn't mean that you are wrong: it may mean that you have considered different issues as being more important than those set out. Ask yourself: 'can I justify my solution?'

Self-assessment

Case study 1: confidentiality

Your pharmacy issues receipts to every customer who brings in a prescription to collect at a later time or date. You are approached by a customer wishing to collect some baby milk on a prescription left earlier that day but the customer does not have the prescription receipt. The pharmacy policy states that sufficient information to enable identification and a signature must be obtained before a supply will be made without the receipt. The customer provides the baby's name, date of birth and correct address and is happy to fill in the back of the prescription.

The next day the child's mother appears with the prescription receipt and asks to collect the milk for the baby. You inform her that you have already supplied and it was collected yesterday. She then contacts the child's father whilst in the shop and finds out that the milk was collected by the father's new partner. She becomes very angry and demands to know why the milk was given to the father's partner and not to her. What should you do?

Case study 2: abusive customer

You are the pharmacist in a pharmacy with a separate medicines counter. A young man approaches the counter and is abusive to your medicines counter assistant. You go to assist the member of staff. The customer is then abusive to you and demands his prescription. Would you serve the customer or not?

Case study 3: complaints

A man approaches you in the pharmacy presenting a medicine bottle dispensed by a different local pharmacy. It is labelled as containing 100 ml and contains what appears to be an antibiotic liquid. He asks you for advice, saying it looks funny and he does not think he should take it. The customer agrees to let you examine it further and you find that the bottle has been filled to the very top. With the customer's consent you pour the bottle into a measuring cylinder. You find that it contains approximately 120 ml of liquid and you notice that there are some white flakes floating in the liquid. You know that these are not normally part of the antibiotic preparation even when reconstituted. The customer then asks what you can do to help him and how he can make a complaint about the other pharmacist. How do you react?

Case study 4: dispensing errors

You work as one of three pharmacists in a very busy pharmacy that dispenses approximately 16 000 items a month. You have noticed that your pharmacy is making a dispensing error at a rate of approximately 1 per week. When reviewing the errors you notice that everyone who works there has made an error and that no one of the dispensing staff is making significantly more errors than the others. You do however discover that one of the pharmacists is responsible for most of the errors that reach the patients. What should you do?

Case study 5: veterinary supply, or not
You are working as a locum pharmacist when a customer approaches you and asks to buy a pot of 500 chlorpheniramine 4 mg tablets. He says these are for his capuchin monkey who suffers from an allergy. The customer tells you he has bought them before. What will you do?

Case study 6: disabled access
Your pharmacy has recently been refitted and the dispensary is now on a raised platform approximately 20 cm off the ground towards the back of the sales floor. This has improved visibility of the shop floor for the pharmacist and improved confidentiality by making it more difficult for customers to view the activity carried on within the dispensary. A regular customer who is a wheelchair user has approached you in the shop area to discuss his access with you. Due to the fact there is no ramp up to the dispensary he finds that since the refit he cannot manoeuvre his chair close enough to speak to the pharmacy staff. He tells you he will have to use another pharmacy in future. What should you do?

Case study 7: police visit
You are the pharmacist in charge. You are serving customers at your medicines counter when a police officer approaches and asks you for information about a service user. You know the patient he is asking about; it is one of your current methadone patients. You are informed that the patient has died in suspicious circumstances and that the police officer wants to look at the patient's medication record and your controlled drug register. The officer tells you that he cannot give you any further information. Would you allow the officer to view your register?

Case study 8: overseas prescriber
A customer approaches the pharmacy counter and presents a prescription written in a foreign language. She asks in broken English for the prescription to be dispensed. When you enquire where the prescription is from, you discover that she is German and in Britain to pursue her studies in English. She said that her doctor had told her that since England is part of the European Union she should be able to get her prescription dispensed here. Neither you nor any of your staff read or speak German. What should you do to try and assist her?

Case study 9: dog wormers

A customer approaches the counter and asks for a worming treatment for his dog. The customer knows the breed of the dog but not how much it weighs. You are a locum pharmacist and admit that you have little experience relating to the provision of veterinary medicines. What should you do?

KeyPoints

There is often no one correct answer to problems in pharmacy practice. Much will depend on the specific circumstances of the case, the experience and knowledge of the individual pharmacist and any support staff.

Use a decision-making framework to help ensure that you have covered the situation from all angles and consider making a contemporaneous written record of the justification.

Case study 10: controlled drug balance

You are working in a company pharmacy as a locum. The pharmacy does not have a manager and it appears that no one is in charge. You are booked to work at the pharmacy for one day each week for the next month. During the course of the first day you identify that the running balance in the controlled drug register appears to be wrong for a number of different drugs. What should you do?

Further reading

Wingfield J, Badcott D. *Pharmacy Ethics and Decision Making*. London: Pharmaceutical Press, 2007.

Answers to self-assessment

Chapter 1

1. For criminal action in a prosecution by the state (crown), balance of proof for a trial is beyond reasonable doubt and sanctions can include fines and imprisonment. For civil law an individual sues another, burden of proof in the trial is on balance of probabilities and sanctions can include award of compensatory payments.
2. There are two chambers in the UK Parliament.
3. Government chambers are situated in the Palace of Westminster, London.
4. 646 Members of Parliament sit in the House of Commons.
5. In 2009 Andy Burnham took over from Alan Johnson as Secretary for State for Health.
6. There are six health ministers in the main government department.
7. In 2009 the Health Minister with responsibility for pharmacy was Mike O'Brian.
8. Chief professional officer posts include the chief medical officer (in 2009 Prof. Sir Liam Donaldson); the chief pharmaceutical officer (in 2009 Dr Keith Ridge); the chief nursing officer (in 2009 Dame Christine Beasley); the chief scientific officer (in 2009 Prof. Sue Hill); the chief public health officer (in 2009 Karen Middleton); and the chief dental officer (in 2009 Barry Cockcroft).

Chapter 2

1. The various stages a new drug has to go through in order to obtain a marketing authorisation are: preclinical research and testing, phases I, II and III clinical trials, each with increasing numbers of participants.
2. c. The quantity of medicinal product in the container is not a legal requirement on the label of a dispensed medicine.
3. c. The age, not the date of birth, of the patient is only required if the patient is aged under 12 years. In many cases the date of birth is included, particularly on computer-generated prescriptions, although this is not legally required.
4. c. A doctor, pharmacist and nurse must sign a patient group direction for the supply of a POM.
5. b. A manufacturer's packet containing 50 paracetamol 500 mg tablets is a POM medicine.
6. c. A medicine made in the pharmacy from ingredients that are all GSL is a P medicine.

7. The following records must be maintained under the 'responsible pharmacist' regulations:
- the name and registration number of the responsible pharmacist
- date and time that person became the responsible pharmacist
- date and time that person ceased to be the responsible pharmacist
- date and time any absence began and ceased.

8. **b.** A responsible pharmacist must be appointed to cover all the hours that a pharmacy is open for business.

9. **d.** An emergency supply cannot be made of a POM at the request of a patient who has previously been prescribed the item by a dentist registered in the USA.

10. **b.** A supplementary prescriber may prescribe within the guidelines set out in the clinical management plan.

Chapter 3

1. The Veterinary Medicines Regulations are revoked and remade each year.

2. The remade regulations commence on 1 October.

3. The letters VMP stand for veterinary medicinal product.

4. A VMP is defined as: 'any substance or combination of substances presented as having properties for treating or preventing disease in animals, or any substance that may be used in or administered to animals to restore, correct or modify physiological functions by exerting a pharmacological, immunological or metabolic action, or making a medical diagnosis' (Veterinary Medicines Regulations 2008).

5. POM-V: prescription-only medicine – veterinarian can only be supplied against a valid veterinary prescription by a veterinarian or pharmacist.
    POM-VPS: prescription-only medicine – veterinarian, pharmacist, suitably qualified person can also only be supplied against a valid veterinary prescription but includes supply by a suitably qualified person in addition to supply by either a veterinary surgeon or a pharmacist. For both of these categories the prescription requirements are the same and a record must be made of the supply; this record is then retained for a minimum of 5 years.
    NFA-VPS: non-food-producing animal – veterinarian, pharmacist, suitably qualified person medicines do not require a prescription or records of receipt or supply need to be made, although it is considered good practice to do so. Sale or supply is restricted to veterinarians, pharmacists and suitably qualified persons.
    AVM-GSL: authorised veterinary medicine – General Sales List have no restrictions on their sale.

6. The requirements for a legally valid prescription for a POM for veterinary use are as for human medicines but also need to include the following: the telephone number of the prescriber; the name and address of the animal's keeper; the address at which the animal is normally kept if this is not the owner's address; the species of animal; its identification and, if a herd, the number of animals being treated; the amount of product being prescribed; and the withdrawal period if relevant.

7. Records of veterinary medicines dispensed must be kept for 5 years and should contain the following: date; name of the VMP; the batch number; the quantity

supplied; the name and address of the recipient; and a copy of the prescription, including the name and address of the prescriber.

8. When supplying under the prescribing cascade the pharmacist must satisfy him- or herself that the words 'under the cascade' appear on the prescription, which has been authorised by a veterinary surgeon under whose care the animal has been placed.

9. The labelling requirements for VMPs dispensed against a prescription not under the cascade are as follows: there is no legal requirement to label, although it is good professional practice to label with date of supply, name and address of supplier, and name and address of recipient.

10. The maximum period of validity for a veterinary controlled drug prescription under the Misuse of Drugs Regulations 2001 is 28 days.

Chapter 4

1. **d.** Phenobarbital does not require safe custody; all of the other drugs fall under the safe custody regulations, including midazolam.

2. **b.** Police officers were provided with powers by the Home Office under the Defence of the Realm Act 1914. Whilst the Dangerous Drugs Act 1920 widened the remit of inspection, senior police officers have been able to inspect pharmacies since 1917.

3. **a.** The prescription requirements for schedule 2 controlled drugs include the requirement that the quantity is written in words and figures.
■   Private prescription forms for controlled drugs in Scotland are beige.
■   Veterinary surgeons do not have to use a standardised prescription form at present.
■   Prescriptions for controlled drugs are valid for 28 days only.
■   Prescriptions can and do request more than 30 days' supply; 30 days is currently only guidance.

4. **b.** Schedule 3 controlled drug stock must be destroyed in the presence of an authorised witness if the safe custody regulations apply to that drug.
    In large chain pharmacies the non-pharmacist managers are often trained and authorised to destroy out-of-date controlled drugs stock.

5. **c.** The Home Office department has indicated that it considers that the words 'one to be taken as directed' to be a satisfactory dose instruction, although the words 'as directed' on their own would not be. 'Tab' is considered to be a satisfactory form on a controlled drug prescription, although the letter 'T' alone would not be, and the quantity must be present in words and figures.

6. **c.** Misuse of Drugs Regulations 2006 as amended is not current legislation under the Misuse of Drugs Act 1971. The regulations were subject to considerable amendment in 2006 but the 2001 regulations were not replaced.

7. **c. i.** False – a prescription for schedule 2 controlled drugs can legally be written for more than 30 days' clinical need; this requirement is good practice but not a legal requirement. **ii.** True – a prescription for schedule 2 controlled drugs must be dated and is only valid for 28 days from that date, or the specified instalment start date.

8.   **d.** A record of supply does not have to be made in the controlled drug register in relation to a prescription for temazepam, a schedule 3 controlled drug.
9.   **c.** All schedule 2 and some schedule 3 controlled drug medicines may need to be kept in a controlled drug cabinet.
10. **b.** A controlled drug register for schedule 2 controlled drugs must be kept for at least 2 years from the last entry and 5 years if this was a veterinary prescription.

Chapter 6

1.   **d.** Private doctors; these do not have an NHS contract to provide medical services.
2.   **a.** Prescription-based interventions; the other services listed are essential or enhanced.
3.   **d.** Signposting; the other services listed are advanced or enhanced.
4.   **a.** Permission of the patient's general practitioner to undertake a medicines use review – it's the pharmacist's decision to offer this service.
5.   **c.** 60 years; the NHS came into being in 1948.
6.   **a.** Medicines use review; the others (reviewing medicines usage, medicines usage review, review of medicine use) are not correct names for the NHS service.
7.   **c.** England and Wales – Scotland and Northern Ireland have their own separate contractual arrangements.
8.   **d.** Primary care groups; this is the old name for the predecessors of primary care trusts in England and health boards in Wales and Scotland. Primary care groups no longer exist.
9.   **b.** Drug Tariff: this is the monthly publication from the NHS that provides details of payments under the pharmacy contractual framework in England and Wales.
10. **a.** General nurse services: nurses are employed by the NHS but are not primary care contractors.

Chapter 7

1.   **d.** Under the risk assessment process it is important to record what you have identified and act on the improvements you could make to demonstrate an ongoing commitment to health and safety.
2.   **c.** Use of industrial denatured alcohol (IDA) for extemporaneous dispensing of NHS prescriptions does not have to be recorded for excise duty purposes. (Completely denatured alcohol is usually purple in colour, IDA sales are limited to 20 litres and trade-specific denatured alcohol is used in the cosmetic/cleaning and printing industries.)
3.   **a.** Requirements for safety symbols are included in the CHIP regulations.
4.   **c.** Part I poisons can only be sold by pharmacists.
5.   **b.** Pharmacies can only store hazardous waste for 6 months.
6.   **c.** The limit on waste was increased from 200 kg per year to 500 kg per year.
7.   **c.** Pharmacies with 5 staff or more must display a health and safety poster. (Accidents covered by RIDDOR must be reported by telephone immediately and in writing within 10 days and all workplaces must give employees some basic health and safety training.)

8. **b.** Police officers requesting information need to make the request in writing, signed by an officer. (Coroners can demand confidential information, very young children do not understand the concept of informed consent, the teenager has given consent and so this is not an issue, and it should not be assumed that mentally disabled patients cannot give consent and the request should be reviewed on a case-by-case basis.)

9. **c.** Patients taking multiple medicines may not be able to manage their medication effectively and a compliance tray may be necessary or appropriate, although not always so. (Patients with memory problems may benefit from reminder charts and alarms; patients with impaired vision may benefit from large-print labels or a compliance tray; and patients with poor manual dexterity may benefit from non-child-resistant lids, winged caps or a compliance tray.)

10. **b.** Pharmacists are not required to make major physical changes to their premises, only those that are reasonable to allow access to services.

Chapter 8

1. **a.** The Pharmaceutical Society was established in 1841 by Jacob Bell.
2. **d.** The establishment of a register of practising pharmacists was not an aim of the newly established Pharmaceutical Society.
3. **c.** It become a legal requirement for all practising pharmacists to register with the Pharmaceutical Society in 1933.
4. **c.** The relevant legislation that required this registration was the Pharmacy Act 1933.
5. **d.** The title 'Royal' was granted to the Pharmaceutical Society in 1988.
6. **d.** Maintenance of a benevolent fund for pharmacists and their dependants is not one of the roles and functions of the GPhC.
7. **d.** The Pharmacy Order 2009 is the legislation which governs the operation of the GPhC.
8. **c.** The Law and Ethics Committee is not a relevant committee under the fitness to practise mechanisms.
9. **c.** 5 years from the date of removal is the period of time that must elapse before a person removed from the register is allowed to apply for restoration.
10. **b.** A police caution received in any European country is not considered to be impairment in relation to fitness to practise, although one received in the British Isles would be.

Chapter 9

1. **c.** The Pharmaceutical Society first adopted a Code of Ethics in 1939.
2. **b.** 'Professional services may not be advertised' is not a principle in the Code of Ethics.
3. **d.** 'Patient consent' is not one of Beauchamp and Childress's four basic principles of biomedical ethics.
4. **b.** The word 'non-maleficence' means 'do no harm'.
5. **a.** The individual does not need to be at least 21 years old for informed consent.

6. **d.** Removing dispensing labels from returned medicines and disposing of these in the waste bin would not be a suitable method of disposal for confidential waste.
7. **a.** Concordance is the process of shared decision making between the prescriber and the patient.
8. **c.** Injury caused by failure to follow advice provided is not a necessary element in relation to proving a claim of negligence.
9. **a.** Purchase of a medicine to treat a licensed indication is not a possible reason for intentional misuse of a medicine.
10. **c.** The pharmacist does not need to be directly involved with all sales of medicines that might be misused.

Chapter 10

Case study 1

Issues
- The pharmacy has a duty to ensure that prescription items are delivered to the correct person.
- There has been a possible breach of the Data Protection Act 1998 and Code of Ethics relating to principle 3 and guidance on confidentiality.
- NHS pharmacy contract requires prompt and accurate dispensing.
- What steps were taken to ensure that the person collecting the prescription item was entitled to do so? Was the person known to the pharmacy? What was her relationship to the child?
- If there are domestic problems between the parents, is there a child protection issue in relation to the Children Act 2004?

Prioritise
- You need to ensure that the child will receive the milk as his or her care is your prime concern.
- The pharmacist and staff must abide by the law relating to the protection of data.
- The mother is obviously upset and needs reassurance regarding the safety of her child's medication.

Outcomes
- If the milk has been collected by someone else, will the child receive it?
- If the pharmacy has divulged information about the child improperly there is potential for prosecution under the Data Protection Act.
- If the pharmacy has not followed its standard operating procedures, has a dispensing incident occurred that needs reporting?

Decide/act
- Calm the mother down: listening to her concerns may be as important as resolving them.

- Check your standard operating procedures are accurate, up to date and fit for purpose.
- Check your staff understand and are complying with your standard operating procedures.
- Ensure that the child's mother has sufficient supplies of milk or can obtain the milk from the other parent; if not, consider making a further supply.

Justification

Unfortunately the pharmacist in this case appears to have been caught up in a complicated domestic situation. Legally there are no data protection issues as the pharmacist did not divulge any information. The pharmacist does however have a duty to the patient with regard to dispensing as part of the NHS pharmacy contract.

The pharmacy should have adequate standard operating procedures to ensure that prescriptions are supplied to the right person. In reviewing this case it would be advisable to check that the standard operating procedures are in place and are being followed by staff.

If the standard operating procedures were being followed and are robust then it appears that there is little you could offer to the parent.

The ethical issues of this case are covered by the Code of Ethics and in particular the professional standards and guidance for the sale and supply of medicines. If these standards are being met by the standard operating procedures in place at the pharmacy, then ethically the pharmacist has discharged his or her duties.

To reduce the parent's concerns you could make a note on the baby's medication record that the medication should only be supplied to the mother providing she has legal custody of the child as the child is unable to make his or her own decisions.

In this case apologising for the distress and demonstrating that you are willing to help will probably resolve the situation effectively.

Case study 2

Issues

- The customer is being rude and abusive but you don't know why. If the situation is unresolved the customer may become violent.
- You have a duty under the Health and Safety at Work etc. Act 1974 to protect your staff.
- According to principle 1 of the Code of Ethics you have a duty to the customer to provide NHS pharmaceutical services to patients presenting with a prescription as well as under the NHS contract.
- As your pharmacy is private property you have a legal right to exclude people.

Prioritise

- Your duty of care to the patient means that you cannot deny him his medicines.
- You also have a duty of care to your staff but this must not compromise patient care.
- If you fail to protect your staff adequately, there is a potential for legal action against you.

Outcomes

- You could try to eject the customer from the pharmacy and support your staff.
- You could advise the customer he will not be served unless he alters his behaviour.
- You could advise the customer that you will dispense the prescription but that he must wait outside the pharmacy.
- You could advise the customer that someone else must collect the prescription and that he is not welcome in your pharmacy.

Decide/act

- Any action that involves confronting the customer may lead to further conflict.
- Serving the customer whilst making it clear that you will not tolerate such behaviour is likely to be the best course of action.

Justification

The instant personal reaction may be to try to eject the customer from the store.

It is not an ideal situation to be placed in. Refusing to serve a customer causes an ethical dilemma for pharmacists in that the Code of Ethics states that the patient should be the pharmacist's prime concern. By refusing to serve the customer the risk of verbal abuse or violence to the pharmacist and the member of staff increases. This risk could be further increased if the customer is confronted by the pharmacist or admonished, which causes embarrassment. Talking to other experienced pharmacists or undergoing training may help you to deal with these situations.

Case study 3

Issues

- When reconstituted antibiotic liquids normally contain 100 ml. It appears that the pharmacist who dispensed the item may not have taken the displacement factor into account.
- The white flakes present in the liquid are extraneous and warrant further investigation. They could be some sort of contamination and as such the medicine might be supplied in breach of section 64 of the Medicines Act 1968 which requires the medicine supplied to be of the nature demanded.
- The pharmacy dispensing the product has a duty to provide medicines to the required standard. When was the medicine dispensed and how has it been stored? Is it in date? What is the identity of the dispensing pharmacist?
- Although the customer is not your patient you do have an ethical responsibility to resolve this situation effectively.

Prioritise

- The customer needs to receive a safe and effective medicine, and if this product is substandard a new supply needs to be obtained. Consider what harm can be caused. Can another prescription be obtained? If not, can an emergency supply be made?

- The pharmacy dispensing the product is responsible under section 64 of the Medicines Act 1968 to provide a safe medicine to the required standard.

Outcomes
- If this is not resolved the patient will be left with a substandard treatment.
- You cannot definitively determine whether the service provided by the pharmacy involved is unsafe for patients. However if concerns have been raised it would be advisable to share those concerns.

Decide/act
- Your first concern would be to help the patient to get the medication he needs; this may involve contacting the prescriber yourself or directing the patient back to the prescriber. As a minimum he should be directed back to the dispensing pharmacy to have the antibiotic dispensed again. Once this has been resolved then a complaint should be considered. If none of this is possible, consider making an emergency supply.

Justification
The patient needs the medication and this must be your priority. However from the appearance of the product presented it seems that a dispensing error has been made and the standards of manufacture in the supplying pharmacy could be substandard. The pharmacy involved may also be in breach of essential services 1 and 8 of the pharmacy contract.

The patient has asked for advice on how to complain about the pharmacist. Initially he should be referred to the supplying pharmacist to give the pharmacist the opportunity to apologise, resolve the complaint and change procedures if needed. However if this does not resolve the issue then you could advise the patient to contact the professional regulator. If you have further concerns about the pharmacy you may consider contacting the regulator yourself.

Case study 4

Issues
- Official guidance on this issue includes guidance on whistle blowing, Code of Ethics principles 1, 2 and 7 and common-law duty of care, quality of service and patient safety.
- There is a problem with dispensing errors in this pharmacy that cannot be left without investigation.
- If the pharmacy blames individuals for errors, it is likely that errors will go unreported and the service will not improve.
- There is a need to identify whether there has been a change in business levels, footfall or staffing levels to determine whether external factors are affecting the level of dispensing errors.

Prioritise
- It is never satisfactory to allow dispensing errors to reach the patient.

- The problem is one that needs to be dealt with by all dispensary staff.
- The pharmacists involved needs to review their dispensing and checking processes.
- The pharmacy and the staff employed need to review their processes as a whole to try and reduce the error rate.
- If patient safety continues to be an issue will you need to whistleblow.

Outcomes

- If nothing is done the errors will continue. If you are aware of a problem and may be able to have an effect but take no action then you are compounding the problem. The pharmacist responsible for the most errors that reach the patient should be advised to review his or her procedures and take appropriate action.
- The pharmacy team as a whole should review internal and external factors that may affect errors and make changes where necessary. Under essential service 8, dispensing errors should be reported to the National Patient Safety Agency.

Decide/act

- Review internal and external factors that may affect error rates in the pharmacy. A no-blame culture will make the staff more likely to share concerns. Tools such as root cause analysis may be beneficial in resolving errors. Staff should review their own processes and a period of observation may help. If this does not resolve the underlying problem then further investigation of the pharmacist may be appropriate, reporting the pharmacist to your superintendent pharmacist, the owner or even to the professional regulator.
- Determine the types of error that have occurred and where possible when they occurred. This will help you to determine whether the time of day was a factor and therefore if you need to change your staffing profile. If a particular type of error is occurring this might indicate that the layout of the dispensary needs to be changed or that there is a particular training need in the pharmacy.

Justification

The error rate in the pharmacy is around 1 item in every 4000 dispensed. This is not a particularly high error rate but should be cause for concern. Firstly all staff including yourself should be assessed to ensure compliance with the standard operating procedures.

If one of the pharmacists is responsible for most of the errors that reach the patient he or she needs to be advised and supported to improve. Simply blaming someone for making mistakes does not reduce the risk of it happening again but it does increase the risk that errors will not be reported in future. The pharmacist involved should be helped to review checking procedures and also supported if there are work or external factors that are affecting this colleague's performance. If the individual fails to improve you will have no choice under the principle of non-maleficence other than to report the matter and the steps taken to try and resolve it to the owner or regulator.

Case study 5

Issues

- Veterinary Medicines Regulations: the medicine appears to be wanted for an animal and not a human. Chlorpheniramine is a pharmacy (P) medicine licensed for use in humans; when used in animals it becomes a prescription-only medicines – veterinarian, pharmacist, suitably qualified person (POM-VPS), so if being used for animal treatment a prescription is required. The medicine is not a licensed veterinary medicinal product for animal use and no indication is given. Is a suitable licensed veterinary product available?
- Was the product previously obtained from this pharmacy without a prescription? If so, when?
- Professional standards and guidance on the sale of medicines, section 2, should be consulted.
- The quantity requested is high. Would use of this product for a long period be justified?
- Can the product be misused and if so, is this likely?

Prioritise

- Whilst the animal is not a human, you still have a duty to provide care.
- The pharmacist must act within his or her competence and knowledge.
- The pharmacist must abide by the law relating to the sale of medicines.
- Antihistamines are known to have been purchased for reasons of misuse or abuse.

Outcomes

- Refusing to supply could deny the patient care, even if the patient is an animal.
- Supplying the medicine is illegal under the Veterinary Medicines Regulations and could result in the pharmacist being prosecuted.
- Uncontrolled sales of medicines liable to misuse can be considered misconduct and referred to the regulator for consideration of fitness to practise.

Decide/act

- The pharmacist should refuse the sale and direct the owner to a vet who can write a prescription for the medicine 'under the cascade'. This will enable the owner to obtain treatment legally; however it may result in the owner incurring additional costs.

Justification

The medicine cannot be legally supplied over the counter as it is for an animal and therefore requires a prescription. The owner may have made the request because the product is cheaper to buy in bulk than buying proprietary packs or obtaining the product on prescription.

Case study 6

Issues
- You have a responsibility to provide services as part of your NHS pharmacy contract.
- You have a responsibility to provide access to the patient under the Disability Discrimination Act 1995 and 2005.
- Was disabled access considered when the pharmacy was refitted?

Prioritise
- The customer must be able to access the pharmacy; action must be taken either to allow access or to provide a suitable alternative.
- You have a legal duty to take reasonable steps to provide access to services for disabled customers.
- If one patient is experiencing these difficulties, others may also be.

Outcomes
- If you do nothing you are denying the patient access to services and leaving yourself open to potential litigation.
- Your pharmacy has just been refitted. Is it possible or financially viable to make changes to the pharmacy?
- Will discussion of the customer's needs help to resolve the issue?

Decide/act
- Talking to the patient to determine his needs would be a good place to start. Low-cost options such as putting a bell in the lower area or allowing the customer to phone the pharmacy so a member of staff can meet him on the shop floor would meet both the customer's needs and your obligations under the Disability Discrimination Acts.

Justification
Small changes affecting access can make major differences to patients' lives. The Disability Discrimination Act protects the rights of individuals and also allows businesses to make common-sense decisions to improve access to services that don't have to cost vast amounts of money. Ethically you have a duty of care to the patient. However from a practical point of view the cost of a phone call or a push-button bell will be more than outweighed by the loss of business and bad public relations that a negative headline in a local paper can cause.

Case study 7

Issues
- Relevant guidelines include the Data Protection Act and associated legislation, Code of Ethics principle 3 and professional standards and guidance for patient confidentiality.
- The police officer is investigating a potential crime and has asked for your help.

- Despite the patient being deceased you still have a duty with regard to confidentiality.
- The patient has not given, and apparently now is not able to give, consent to disclose such information.
- The police do not have an automatic right to inspect pharmacy and patient records. Showing the officer your records could affect the confidentiality of other patient data.
- Consider whether there is a risk of harm to the public that outweighs any confidentiality owed to the patient.

Prioritise
- Whilst pharmacists should assist the police they also have a duty of confidentiality to the patient involved and also other patients with records in the register. Is the police officer requesting the information or disclosure covered by the exceptional circumstances set out in the professional guidance?

Outcomes
- If the police need access to the records they can make a request in writing stating the purpose. If however the coroner had requested the information, the pharmacist would have to divulge the minimum information needed to comply with the court order or be deemed in contempt of court.
- If the pharmacist did give the police officer full access to records then an offence may have been committed under the Data Protection Act.

Decide/act
- Full access to the records is inappropriate and unnecessary.
- It would be sensible to ask the police to make a request for access in writing rather than just refuse. Limited access, such as making a list of records or photocopying the record and deleting other patients' details, would be a sensible option if a written request is received.

Justification
The Code of Ethics and professional standards guidance require pharmacists to protect patients; it is possible to protect the information held on patients without obstructing the police in their investigations. The police officer is unlikely to understand your predicament, so being open and honest about your duty to the patient may help. A balance must be struck so that confidentiality is not compromised and the police can investigate a potential crime effectively.

Case study 8

Issues
- The customer has a prescription issued in the European Economic Area (EEA) and prescriptions written by authorised doctors and dentists from the EEA are valid for dispensing in Britain.
- The patient can communicate in basic English. You cannot speak German.

- The prescription is written in German and unless you are competent in relation to interpreting the prescription and in your knowledge of German medicines (medicines do not always have the same ingredients in different countries), can you safely dispense the prescription? Principles 1 and 2 of the Code of Ethics are relevant.
- Clinical knowledge – what is the prescription for and is it urgent?

Prioritise

- Is the prescriber registered in the EEA? Contact details for registering bodies in the EEA are available on the internet from the Royal Pharmaceutical Society of Great Britain website (www.rpsgb.org.uk).
- You have a duty of care to the patient with regard to the prescription. This means that you cannot dispense if this would be associated with a possibility of harm due to lack of comprehension. You also need to find a suitable alternative source of help for the patient.
- Ethically, if you are not competent in the language of the patient, you should question whether you are competent to dispense and advise on the dispensed medicine.
- Can another pharmacy help?

Outcomes

- Refuse to dispense the prescription. If you cannot read the prescription then it would not be safe to dispense.
- What would happen to the patient if she does not have any medication?
- Direct the customer to another health professional. Do you know someone who does speak German? Could the prescription be rewritten by a local doctor?

Decide/act

- If you were able to read the prescription and are confident in your knowledge of German prescribed medicines and ability to dispense, then you could dispense the prescription privately.
- If you feel you are not competent, you cannot dispense the item but must explain the problem to the patient.

Justification

As the safety of the patient is your prime concern, dispensing a prescription when you are unsure of the information written is unethical. It would be less risky to signpost the patient to another healthcare professional who could reassess the patient's needs and provide a British prescription. Making a mistake would cause more potential harm to the patient. This example demonstrates that pharmacists need to be aware of the skills and attributes of other pharmacists and healthcare professionals in their area so that signposting of patients is effective and not simply a means of dealing quickly with difficult situations.

Case study 9

Issues
- Relevant guidelines include Veterinary Medicines Regulations and Code of Ethics.
- Despite the fact that this is an animal, you have a duty of care under the Code of Ethics. However you must also be sure that you are competent with regard to any service provided.
- There are numerous products available for treating worms in animals which are available to purchase in pharmacies. Treatment is dependent on the size of the dog, so knowledge of how to use the product safely is necessary to enable the sale to go ahead.

Prioritise
- The owner wishes to treat the dog for intestinal worms. Although not an immediately life-threatening condition, failure to treat will lead to further symptoms and cause the animal unnecessary suffering.
- In addition, if the animal is not treated and is in contact with humans then there is a risk of transferring the parasite to a human host, resulting in illness.
- If the wrong product is sold and the treatment is subtherapeutic the parasitic infection will remain.
- If an overdose is given then side-effects may occur which can be serious.
- Any harm caused to the animal as a result of your recommendation could result in a claim for negligence.

Outcomes
- Refuse the sale as you are not competent to make the sale.
- Refer the customer to a vet or another pharmacy that sells these products.
- Ask staff in the pharmacy if they have been trained in selling the product. Are any of your medicine counter assistants competent to make the sale under your supervision?

Decide/act
- If there is a member of staff who is competent in the sale of these products, then he or she will be able to assist you in determining which treatment is appropriate. This will allow the owner to purchase the correct product to treat the animal. Failing this, direct the customer to an alternative source of help.

Justification
Pharmacy staff are usually trained to be able to sell products to suitable customers. Whilst worming treatments are for animals, the methods of determining appropriateness of treatment used for human medicines should equally apply. If the member of staff clearly demonstrates to you his or her competence in determining

whether the treatment is appropriate and can demonstrate the rationale to you there is no reason why the sale should not go ahead.

Case study 10

Issues
- Relevant guidelines include Misuse of Drugs Regulations 2001 as amended, Responsible Pharmacist Regulations 2008 and NHS contract – clinical governance.
- Running balances are not a legal requirement for controlled drugs but an error in this may indicate other issues relating to the lawful supply of controlled drugs. These could include pharmacist failure to record purchases or supplies, an incorrect entry being made in the register therefore affecting the balance or, in the worst case, theft.
- As the responsible pharmacist you are responsible for meeting the requirement to have standard operating procedures in place.

Prioritise
- If you do nothing the discrepancy in the register will remain. If theft or any failures with regard to requirements of the Misuse of Drugs Regulations are suspected in the future then you may become a suspect as the register was incorrect when you worked in that pharmacy.
- Reviewing the register may result in you finding a dispensing error made by a previous pharmacist. If there is a mistake in the register this would have to be rectified and the owner and/or superintendent pharmacist informed.

Outcomes
- Do nothing and leave the problem for someone else to sort out – this is not an acceptable option.
- Review the contents of the controlled drug cupboard and reconcile the register, making an entry to reconcile any discrepancy.
- Report any discrepancies to the pharmacy owner and superintendent pharmacist so that they can keep the matter under review.

Decide/act
- The running balance must be reconciled and any discrepancy recorded. This may result in the identification of mistakes made by other pharmacists. If these mistakes are simple data entry errors they will be easy to reconcile. If entries have been missed or potential theft has occurred, then advice may need to be sought.

Justification
You are the pharmacist in charge on the day you are present in that pharmacy; as such you are responsible for everything that occurs during that day. Failure to act could lead to you becoming involved in an investigation if a serious problem arises. The owner and other pharmacists could claim that the balance was correct when they

left and that you may be responsible for the discrepancy. For your own safety and that of the public it would be beneficial to check the running balance on each separate occasion you are in the pharmacy.

Significant differences in the running balance may indicate theft or fraud that should be investigated. If you are unable to reconcile the running balance then contacting the owner and superintendent will be the next step. The accountable officer at the primary care organisation may also need to be notified. If you are suspicious you may decide you need to seek the help and advice of your local pharmacy inspector.

Useful websites

Association of Police Controlled Drugs Liaison Officers: www.apcdlo.org.uk
Data Protection Act 1998: www.statutelaw.gov.uk; www.opsi.gov.uk
Discrimination Act 1995: www.statutelaw.gov.uk; www.opsi.gov.uk
Defra (government department on environment, food and rural affairs): www.defra.gov.uk
Department of Health: www.dh.gov.uk
Drug scope: www.drugscope.org.uk
Environmental Protection Act 1990: www.statutelaw.gov.uk; www.opsi.gov.uk
Environmental Protection Agency: www.enviroment-agency.gov.uk
European Medicines Agency (EMEA): www.emea.europa.eu
Health and Safety at Work Act 1974 and associated legislation: www.statutelaw.gov.uk; www.opsi.gov.uk
Home Office: www.drugs.homeoffice.gov.uk
Know Britain: www.know-britain.com
Medicines and Healthcare products Regulatory Agency (MHRA): www.mhra.gov.uk
National Office for Animal Health (NOAH): www.noah.co.uk
NHS Business Services Authority: www.nhsbsa.nhs.uk
Office of Public Sector Information: www.opsi.gov.uk
Pharmaceutical Services Negotiating Committee (PSNC): www.psnc.org.uk
Poisons Act 1972: www.statutelaw.gov.uk; www.opsi.gov.uk
Primary care contracting: www.pcc.nhs.uk
RPSGB – audits: www.rpsgb.org
Shipman inquiry, fourth report, available at: www.the-shipman-inquiry.org.uk
UK government, the official website: www.direct.gov.uk
UK Parliament: www.ukparliament.uk
Veterinary Medicines Directorate: www.vmd.gov.uk

Glossary

Act or Act of Parliament	Primary legislation or a statute
Authorised person	A title set up under the Health Act 2006 and the Controlled Drug (Supervision of Management and Use) Regulations 2006. Appointed to ensure the safe use of controlled drugs in the primary care organisation
Bill	Precursor to the development of an Act of Parliament. Once the reigning monarch gives assent to a Bill, it becomes an Act of Parliament
Civil law	Relates to contracts between individuals who can sue for breach of that contract. The court can award damages to the injured party if the defendant is proven guilty 'on the balance of probabilities'
Code of Ethics	A set of rules of conduct along with associated guidance that sets out requirements of professional conduct and standards. Its requirements can be over and above those set out in legislation
Criminal law	Law developed to encourage and support safe and orderly living for all citizens. It is enforced by the state through the criminal courts, magistrates and Crown Courts. The defendant is innocent until proved guilty 'beyond reasonable doubt' and the penalties imposed can be fines or imprisonment
Department of Health (DH)	The government department with specific responsibility for health, including pharmacy. Civil servants working within the DH will prepare Green and White Papers as well as health policy documents. The DH negotiates with the pharmaceutical services' negotiating committee to agree the fees and payments for NHS pharmaceutical services, as set out in the Drug Tariff
Devolved legislation	Legislation that usually relates to only one or sometimes more (for example, England and Wales), but not all, countries within the UK
European Medicines Agency (EMEA)	The European counterpart of the MHRA, the EMEA operates a centralised Europewide marketing authorisation for medicines for human and veterinary (animal) use (Regulation (EC) no. 726/2004)

Fitness to practise	All members must declare annually that they remain fit to practise with no criminal record or other impediment with regard to their ability to practise. Regulatory mechanisms are in place for ensuring that members on a practising register of a health profession are fit to carry out their professional duties and not bring their profession into disrepute
General Pharmaceutical Council (GPhC)	From 2010 the regulatory body for pharmacy in Great Britain
Green Paper	A government consultation or discussion paper during the early stages of development of legislation or policy
Great Britain (GB)	Scotland, England and Wales
Medicines and Healthcare products Regulatory Authority (MHRA)	Organisation established under the Medicines Act 1968 with responsibility for licensing medicines for use in the UK
Medicinal product	Substances or combinations of substances which either prevent or treat disease in human beings or are administered to human beings with a view to making a medical diagnosis or to restore, correct or modify physiological functions in humans
National Health Service (NHS)	The organisation set up in the UK in 1948 to provide free Healthcare to the population
NHS Business Service Authority (NHSBSA)	A special health authority set up by the NHS to deal with business and payment aspects of the organisation. This includes the payment for prescription fees and services
NHS pharmacy contract	The contract setting out the arrangement of and organisation for delivery of pharmaceutical services within the NHS through independent pharmacy contractors
Order	Secondary legislation that sets out how a section of an Act will be implemented
Pharmaceutical Services Negotiating Committee (PSNC)	An organisation representing the interests of pharmacy contractors for the purposes of negotiating payments for nationally based services provided by the membership with the relevant government department, the Department of Health
Primary care organisation (PCO)	The name given to the various organisations responsible for delivering primary healthcare to the local population. In England these are primary care trusts, whilst in Scotland, Wales and Northern Ireland they are health boards
Professional regulator	The organisation responsible for overseeing and enforcing legislation governing a particular profession
Regulations	Statutory instrument or secondary legislation that sets out the rules or directions for implementing sections of an Act or primary legislation

Royal Pharmaceutical Society of Great Britain (RPSGB)	Until 2010 the joint regulatory and professional body for pharmacy in Great Britain
Reserved legislation	Legislation that relates to all countries in the UK
Statute	An Act of Parliament, primary legislation. It may relate to one or more or all countries within the UK
Statutory instrument	Secondary delegated legislation. These can be regulations, orders or directives
United Kingdom (UK)	Northern Ireland, Scotland, England and Wales
Veterinary medicinal product (VMP)	Any substance or combination of substances presented as having properties for treating or preventing disease in animals, or any substance that may be used in or administered to animals to restore, correct or modify physiological functions by exerting a pharmacological, immunological or metabolic action, or making a medical diagnosis
White Paper	Government paper or policy after initial stages of consultation and discussion

Index